ALL ABOUT MONEY

You go into a supermarket, choose a tin of
pineapple, and pay for it. The transaction
appears simple: a metal coin is exchanged
for a tin of fruit. But men and women
have had to grow the fruit. They have
had to guard warehouses, type invoices,
sail ships, pilot planes, mine metal,
manufacture paper, and print labels to
produce the tin of pineapple which you
exchange for a metal coin.
The metal coin is *money* – and without it,
life for everybody would be very
different . . . .

Other *ALL ABOUT* books

ALL ABOUT FOOTBALL

and published by Carousel Books

Jennie Hawthorne

ALL ABOUT MONEY

CAROUSEL EDITOR: ANNE WOOD

CAROUSEL BOOKS
A DIVISION OF TRANSWORLD PUBLISHERS LTD
A NATIONAL GENERAL COMPANY

ALL ABOUT MONEY

A CAROUSEL BOOK 0 552 54026 9

Originally published in Great Britain
by W. H. Allen & Co. Ltd

PRINTING HISTORY

W. H. Allen edition published 1970
Corgi edition published 1973

Carousel Books are published by Transworld Publishers Ltd.,
Cavendish House, 57–59 Uxbridge Road, Ealing, London W.5

Printed in Great Britain by
Fletcher & Son Ltd, Norwich

CONTENTS

[Public Archives of Canada Photo.

'Panning' for Gold in Canada.

1

WHAT IS MONEY?

YOU GO INTO A SUPER-
market, choose a tin of pineapple, and pay for it. The transaction
appears simple: a metal coin is exchanged for a tin of fruit. But
men and women have had to grow the fruit. They have had to
guard warehouses, type invoices, sail ships, pilot planes, mine
metal, manufacture paper, and print labels to produce the tin of
pineapple which you exchange for a metal coin. The metal coin is
money, and without it life for everybody would be very different.

A shopkeeper or the cashier at the cash desk of a supermarket
will exchange cocoa from Nigeria or Ghana, salmon from Russia
or Canada, fruit from Australia or South Africa—all kinds of
goods from all over the world—for the right amount of metal
coins or paper notes.

You *can* offer something other than coins or notes, but will the
shopkeeper take it? That depends on what you offer. A diamond
or a car offered in exchange might look so suspicious that it
would probably result in a call to the police before you left the
shop. The shopkeeper accepts the metal coin or the paper note
because it is *good* money.

Money is something acceptable. But gifts are acceptable too,
and not all gifts are money. Gifts may be goods: cars, radios, or
records. Money is something more. It is something acceptable in

The once-familiar sign outside a pawnbroker's shop.

exchange or payment for debt. This definition is still not enough. You can give a person who knows you and is willing to accept your promise an I.O.U. payable in three months' time. This promise to pay will satisfy your friend in payment of your debt, but he is unlikely to be able to exchange the I.O.U. for goods with anybody else. Because the I.O.U. is not immediately, or universally, or generally acceptable in payment of debt, it cannot be described as 'money'.

The purchase of a tin of pineapple creates a debt with the shopkeeper. The debt is settled with the shopkeeper by offering

The pawnbroker at work.

him a metal coin, the price agreed between you. The shopkeeper does not have to wait for the metal to grow big or ripe or full. The money is immediately acceptable to him and to anybody else to whom he may later offer it.

When you do a week's work your employer pays you not in food or clothes, or in vouchers for food and clothes, but in money. An Act of Parliament in 1701 forbade the payment of wages 'in cloth, victuals, or commodities'. But over 170 years later wages were still paid in goods, by 'truck' as it was called. Housewives in Bilston, Staffordshire, pawned flour to get money to pay their rent. Prescot watchmakers were paid in watches for their work; the watches were passed from hand to hand for less and less in exchange, until they reached the pawnshop.

The system of paying wages in goods rather than money was

finally stopped in the nineteenth century by the Truck Acts, and the work of the Trade Unions. Today an employer pays an agreed sum of money in return for an agreed amount of service. He owes something for the service performed and settles his debt with money. He cannot pay wages by cheque, unless the employee agrees. Cheques are a *claim* to money, but they are not immediately or universally acceptable in payment of debt.

This, then, is what money is: anything which is immediately or universally or generally acceptable for the payment of debt. What is the difference between money and legal tender? Legal tender means any payment that a debtor can legally compel his creditor to accept in payment of his debt. It is money made acceptable by law.

In Britain, bank-notes (£1, £5, and £10) are legal tender up to any amount. 50p pieces can be used for payments not exceeding £10, while 10p and 5p pieces can be used for payments not exceeding £5. Bronze coins ($\frac{1}{2}$p, 1p, and 2p) are legal tender only for payments not exceeding 20p.

2

QUALITIES OF
GOOD MONEY

WHAT MAKES METAL COINS OR paper notes acceptable in payment of debt? To put the question another way, what are the qualities of good money? A Government can declare certain pieces of paper or metal to be the official money of the country. This official money is known as currency, because it 'runs' or 'flows' from hand to hand. Because it has Government backing, it sounds very acceptable. But people may distrust the Government. If so, they will try to change their money very quickly for goods, or for some foreign currency, which is thought to be safer than their own.

Since the Second World War the currencies of even the rich nations have been distrusted from time to time. People have tried to get rid of pounds for dollars, dollars for marks, francs for gold bars; and, immediately after the war, marks for cigarettes.

A Government ruling is not enough on its own to make pieces of metal or paper immediately acceptable in payment of debt. What are the special qualities that good money must have?

First, there is *portability*. Suppose instead of paying for your tin of pineapple with a coin of cupro-nickel or bronze, you had to pay with a great bar of lead which could be moved only with the aid of a tractor or a crane? Would the lead be immediately acceptable in payment of debt?

[*British Museum.*

A fifteenth-century French manuscript shows a man burying coins. This was a common practice in the Middle Ages. Sometimes the owner never came back.

If every time a tin of pineapple was bought or sold the buyer or seller had to exchange a load of lead which couldn't be carried unaided, and which only the richest person had room to store, trade in tins of pineapple would soon stop.

Heavy metal bars have been used in the past as money. Iron was especially used by the Spartans to make the accumulation and transport of wealth difficult. It stopped people becoming millionaires—or robbers!

One of the reasons why it is not easy to rob the Bank of England or Fort Knox (where the United States stores its gold) is that gold is an extremely heavy metal. The vaults which contain gold in the Bank of England have a weight limit of 784 lb. a square foot. More than that, and the gold would collapse through the floors and drop into the sewers below. So the gold is kept in little stacks, eleven bars high but worth nearly half a million pounds. The men who move the stacks wear shoes with reinforced toecaps which can resist without crumpling a weight of up to 1 ton.

Although gold bars lack portability, an essential quality of good money, gold is so generally acceptable among govern-

[*Johnson, Matthey & Co. Ltd.*

Pouring chlorine-refined gold into a holding furnace prior to casting the gold bars.

ments at all times that it is still a very vital part of the money system. But good money must be portable so that it can be carried in a pocket or wallet. It must go inside a money box or cash register.

There have been exceptions. The largest coin in the world is a copper plate measuring 25 inches by 13 inches and weighing over 40 lb. It was issued in Sweden during the sixteenth century when the Swedes had an abundance of copper. Only three specimens of this unwieldy coin exist today. As we can guess, such heavy coins were not easily portable, and could not have been very popular, so in 1660 the Bank of Sweden replaced these copper monsters by paper money. (Sweden thus became the first country in Europe to issue bank-notes, but soon reverted to metal coins. When the

13

Bank of England was set up in 1694 it was the only note-issuing bank in the world.)

On the island of Yap, in the south Pacific, money takes the form of large stones. The biggest, 12 feet across, weighs 5 tons. Smaller stones have a hole in the middle so they can be slotted on poles, carried from place to place, and used for small change.

If by contrast to weighty lead, iron, or copper, money was so light and fragile that it crumpled into shreds after being handled a few times it wouldn't be acceptable either, so the second quality of good money is *durability*. It must last. Good money stands up to a fair amount of wear and tear. Coins made of copper or gold sometimes take 5,000 years to wear out, but such metals are precious today. They are wanted in large amounts for industry. Paper money is therefore used instead.

In Great Britain the Bank of England issues over 8 million notes a day. This is five times as many as are issued daily in Western Germany (population 58 million), and more than are issued to the whole of the United States (population 195 million). The average life of a £1 note, which means the length of time it is in use before being returned to the Bank of England as unfit for further circulation, was nineteen months in 1957 but only eight months in 1966. The average life of the ten-shilling note fell during the same period from six months to five months.

The reason for this drop in life span is that people would no longer tolerate worn or dirty notes. Also, if the population is increasing, there are more people to handle them. In other countries, where there is not such a demand for new bank-notes, the average life span of a note may be as long as two years. They are very portable and fairly durable.

Plastic coins claimed to last for ever have been produced by Imperial Chemical Industries for the Cocos Islands in the Indian Ocean, the only country in the world with an ivory currency. The ivory coins naturally wore out in time, so I.C.I. replaced them with 'wear-proof' coins of an acetal copolymer called Kematal, in red for one rupee and green for the lower denominations.

I.C.I. make quite a lot of coins. Their subsidiary, Imperial

[*Johnson, Matthey & Co. Ltd.*

A range of Johnson Matthey gold bars and a collection of gold coinage from various parts of the world.

Metal Industries, own the historic King's Norton Mint in Warwickshire, the source of 'K.N.' pennies. Although the initials K.N. have not appeared on British coins since 1919, the King's Norton mint still subcontracts for the Royal Mint, usually anonymously, but a K.N. penny was made for British West Africa in 1958.

As well as being *portable* and *durable*, good money needs to be *recognizable*. If diamonds or precious stones were used as money,

[*Johnson, Matthey & Co. Ltd.*

Checking a consignment of 'good delivery' gold bars in the vaults of Johnson Matthey (Bankers) Ltd.

how could people tell the difference between a real diamond and one made of paste? Between an aquamarine and a zircon or sapphire? Imagine a woman wanting to buy a car, and offering for it a rare stone. Before the seller accepts the stone in payment for the car he would have to call in a gem expert who could recognize the stone and estimate its worth. By contrast, a Bank of England note is easily recognizable.

Another quality of good money is that it should be *divisible*. Supposing the expert called in by the car dealer to value the rare stone said it was worth £2,000. If the car price was £1,000, would buyer and seller split the stone into two parts? And if they split it into two equal parts, would the halves be equal to £1,000 each? Two halves do not always equal one whole.

Money must also be *homogeneous*. You decide to share a bottle of full-cream milk. The cream is all at the top. The person who gets the top half of the milk will get more cream than the person who gets the bottom half. Skimmed milk and full-cream milk are different; they are not 'homogeneous'. Money, to be immediately acceptable, must be homogeneous. Any one note must be as acceptable as any similar note, and any one penny must be as acceptable as any other penny.

It is true that coin collectors will pay high sums for particular kinds of coins, usually because these coins are very rare. A lot of people want them and will pay a great deal to get them, just as stamp collectors will pay more than the face value of a stamp because it is rare, and much in demand. But even rare coins, if part of the official currency, are acceptable in exchange or payment of a debt.

Suppose you were a bus conductor and a man offered you, as part of his fare, a 1950 or 1951 George VI penny? There were only 0·3 million and 0·1 million of these coins issued, compared with 121 million pennies in 1938 or 157 million in 1962. Or suppose someone offered you for one of these pennies a 1954 British penny, of which only a small number were struck to test the dies, and all trial pieces were thought to have been destroyed? Recently Paramount International Coin Corporation of Eaglewood, Ohio, turned down £9,000 cash offered by a British coin dealer in Northampton.

But if you were a bus conductor you would accept any of these rare pennies as long as it remained legal currency, no matter what a collector was prepared to pay for it. Good money must be homogeneous. In fact, the 1954 penny had been in use like any other penny, but was retrieved from general circulation.

The last quality of good money is that it should be *stable*. This is the same as saying that its value should not alter much. Imagine the official currency of a country to be sea-shells. Once every six

17

months, a very low tide leaves the shells strewn in thousands across the shore. Next morning they are all swept away by a very high tide for another six months. Would the shells be worth as much when there were thousands of them ready for the picking as they would be when there were only a few?

Some currencies alter such a lot that people change them as soon as they can. Some South American currencies have different values for different purposes. In 1923 in Germany so many marks were needed for a stamp that the stamps were overprinted in millions. It is said that people paid for their dinners before they ate them, in case the price went up before they finished.

When more money is offered or is available for the same amount of goods the price of those goods rises. This is one of the reasons why there is so much stress on productivity. People are asked to produce more goods, so that prices will not rise.

If money is to be fairly stable the supply must be *limited*. Some people argue today that money is too scarce for world trade. On the other hand, money so plentiful that it could be picked up anywhere would not be readily acceptable in exchange for goods or debts.

So the qualities of good, or universally acceptable, money are that it should be portable, durable, homogeneous, divisible, and stable. This last quality means, in the modern world, that the supply of money, in whatever form, must be adequately controlled.

3

THE FUNCTIONS OF MONEY

MONEY CONSISTS OF PIECES of paper or metal which are intrinsically worthless. It is not a ticket to happiness, though it allows a man to be miserable in comfort. Religious communities often take a vow of poverty, but for some people money acts like a magnet. It lures them to do incredible things, good or bad. Why has money this fascination?

The answer is that money commands power. It buys goods, and in societies which respect wealth it buys respect. This purchasing power makes money different from all other goods. Goods are wanted for themselves: to eat, drink, look at, touch, work upon. But except for misers like Silas Marner who like to gloat over gold, people want money not for its own sake but for what it can buy.

One of the functions of money is therefore as a *medium of exchange*. People are willing to accept pieces of metal or paper in exchange for goods or services. The pieces of metal used as money in early times were themselves valuable, and it was easy to see a relationship between the value of the metal and the goods offered in exchange. Today the notes or coins may be intrinsically almost worthless. But people accept paper or metal in return for goods and services because they know that they will be able to exchange it for goods and services they also need.

Paying toll to pass over a bridge. This was a usual custom in the Middle Ages.

The second function of money is to serve as a *unit of account*. We can judge the dearness or cheapness of goods by using money. We know an item such as a blanket costing £5 will need more of our money than an item costing £1; we know a wage of £25 per week will get us more services and goods than a wage of £15.

But if our only unit of money was the pound sterling or the dollar we could not compare the value of one item against that of another with much precision. Imagine having to measure the length and breadth of this page if your only unit of measurement was the foot or the metre. In order to get results which mean anything we have to subdivide each foot into inches and each metre into centimetres (and millimetres). For the same reason we divide each £1 into pence and each dollar into cents. Then we can compare the value of one commodity with that of any other commodity fairly accurately.

The third function of money is as a *store of value*. Unlike perishable goods, which spoil or rot away over time, money must preserve its value so that £1 or one dollar today can still be

[*Radio Times Hulton Picture Library.*

A drawing of the Old Toll Bar in London. The Bridge was built in 1769, and removed in 1785.

exchanged for goods and services in the future. The modern banking system has helped to ensure that money does not lose its value with time; but even so, this third function of money, namely to serve as a store of value, is not as efficient today as it once was. If prices rise more than wages do, then money buys less in the future. People who have saved money find that their saved money buys fewer goods. For this reason there is a temptation today for rich people to turn their money into things like Old Master paintings which can be relied on to gain in value as time goes by. Remedies must be found to keep the value of money as constant,

21

or unchanging, as possible, otherwise certain groups of people will be unfairly rewarded or penalized.

The fourth function of money is that it should serve as a standard by which payments may be made in the future—in other words, a *standard of deferred payments*. This is a very important function in modern society. Buying and selling often have to be undertaken before a commodity actually goes on to the market. Rubber takes some years to grow, sugar and cocoa take some months. Contracts may need to be drawn up before the crop matures (and indeed such contracts are known as 'futures'). If £1 (or one dollar) has a very different value in the future from what it has today the function of money as a standard of deferred payments is lost.

This is why inflation (see page 87) which alters the internal value of money in a country, and devaluation (see page 98), which alters the foreign exchange value of money, must be guarded against.

4

HOW MONEY BEGAN

ALTHOUGH MONEY IS CHIEFLY used for trading purposes today, and trade is a very ancient human activity, there are two activities which are even older. Marriage is one, and revenge is another. Both of these played a large part in the development of money.

Early peoples soon found that too much inter-marriage within the tribal family was not good. It was desirable to choose a wife from some group other than their own immediate family or tribe. At certain times of the year, when the rains were plentiful and the search for food and water was eased, great gatherings of nomadic peoples took place. Sometimes girls of equal beauty would be exchanged without further payment; more often one family would need to add a gift with their daughter to make the bargain equal. Those who had no daughter to exchange would need to find the 'bride-price' in some primitive form of money, such as salt, or shells, or plumed head-dresses. A 'head' of cowrie shells in Nigeria contained 2,000 shells, and was worth about five pence. Several 'heads' would be required to buy even a plain wife. Sometimes the price was not paid until the first child of the marriage was born.

Revenge is sweet, says an old proverb, and the 'avengers of blood' are a very old institution. 'An eye for an eye, and a tooth

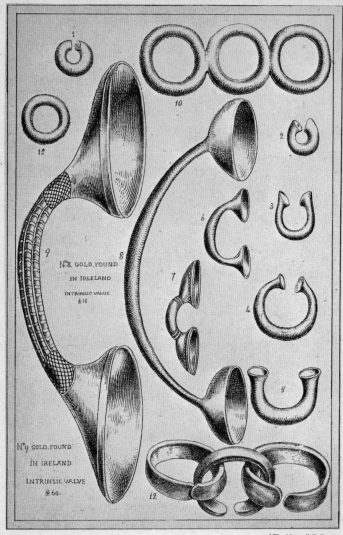

Within the illustration:

N°8. GOLD. FOUND IN IRELAND INTRINSIC VALUE £15

N°9 GOLD. FOUND IN IRELAND INTRINSIC VALUE £60.

[*The Mansell Collection.*

Specimens of the Ring Money of Ireland.

for a tooth' was the old rule. The deliberate killing of a member of the tribe would be avenged by a party of 'avengers of blood' who would swear an oath not to rest content until the death had been repaid. Gradually this revenge was made unnecessary by the

24

payment of compensation in the form of acceptable goods, which became primitive money payments. In Cambodia 30 grammes of silver was paid for a healthy woman, more for a man. If the killing was accidental the payment was reduced to one-third. In New Guinea a man killed in a brawl was worth two good shell arm rings and two good nose sticks. These were also made of shell. Sometimes 'bride money' was connected with 'blood-money' through the mother of the dead person. A son killed in a border dispute was worth whatever amount his father had paid as bride-price for the boy's mother years before. These bride-prices were remembered exactly.

Because we use coin and notes so often, it is hard to think that there was ever a time when payment for debt took place without them. But the Ancient Egyptians are believed to have had a

[*Radio Times Hulton Picture Library.*

Trading at Tidore.

moneyless society: their workers were paid in goods and food rations.

Robert Owen, who after twenty-five years of effort, helped to reduce children's working hours to sixty-nine a week, started a

'London Exchange Bazaar' in 1831, where members could exchange their produce by labour time-notes. Produce was valued by the time spent making it. Perhaps Robert Owen's workers preferred the feel of 'real' money in their hands, for the system failed and Owen had to find £2,000 to foot the bill.

The earliest traders tried barter, i.e. trading one commodity for another. Phoenicians offered their purple cloth for Cornish tin. Africans took beads or salt and gave food, or acted as guides in return. Barter still takes place today. People swap stamps or picture cards. Some countries, with a strict control on the amount of money that leaves their shores, swap goods. Such modern barter has a money value, however, unlike primitive barter, where there was no common measure or standard for judging the value of goods.

Men and women may be used in barter deals. Gerald Brooke, a British lecturer serving a five-year prison sentence in Russia for distributing anti-Soviet literature, was released in exchange for two Russian spies, Peter and Helen Kroger, who were being held by the British.

This example shows one of the difficulties of barter. It needs what is known as a *double coincidence of wants*. Britain wanted Brooke's release just at the very same time that Russia wanted to recover the Krogers.

The second difficulty of barter is *measurement*. How do you measure the value of one thing against the value of another? To exchange Phoenician cloth for Cornish tin was not so hard when there was little else to exchange except tin or cloth. Wants and goods were few. But exchanging the millions of goods produced in the modern world is a very different matter. Money acts as a standard of value, and gives each of those goods a price.

The third difficulty of barter is like the second: if a thing cannot be easily measured it cannot be easily divided. A tailor and a shoemaker may decide to exchange an overcoat for shoes. How do they do it? One overcoat, which is all the shoemaker wants, and all that the tailor is willing to trade, is worth less than two pairs of shoes but more than one pair. The mid-way point of three

British Museum.

Coins of the Sassanian Dynasty of Persia (A.D. 224–651).

1. Gold stater of Ardashir I (224–241).
2. Drachm of Shapur I (241–272).
3. Drachm of Hormizd I (272–273).
4. Drachm of Bahram I (273–276).
5. Drachm of Bahram II (276–293).
6. Gold stater of Narseh (293–303).
7. Drachm of Hormizd II (303–310).
8. Gold stater of Shapur II (310–379).
9. Drachm of Shapur III (383–388).
10. Drachm of Bahram IV (388–399).
11. Drachm of Jamasp (497–499).
12. Drachm of Khusru II (591–628).
13. Drachm of Boran (queen, 630–631).

| National Tourist Organization of Greece.

Excavations around the Palace of Minos (1600–1450 B.C.) on the island of Crete. This is the site of the legend of the Minotaur.

shoes is unsatisfactory to both parties, yet it may have to be accepted, for the nearest alternative is either one or two pairs, and the overcoat can hardly be cut up.

The division of living things has special disadvantages. If two sacks of corn are worth a cow, what is one sack of corn worth?

Finally, barter has the disadvantage that it cannot be easily deferred, that is, put off to a later date. The peasant, with eggs and butter to sell, must find a buyer today, or his journey to market has been wasted. The eggs will be bad, and the butter rancid, by next market day. This makes the peasant more inclined to strike a bargain, even if the exchange is not very fair, for fear the goods are left on his hands.

Because of the difficulties of barter, a new system arose. In early times cows and oxen were greatly desired and acceptable to most people in payment for goods and services. They became a form of money. A 'pecuniary' gain means a 'money' gain and comes from the Latin word *pecus*, meaning 'cattle'. This was a big step in the development of money.

|Coins Weekly.

Reverse of Drachma with the Labyrinth of
Daedalus.

Cows and oxen became generally acceptable in payment of
debt. Many other things have been used as money in different
parts of the world at different times: some are listed in the table
below.

Unusual items which have been used as money	
Beads	Parts of Africa and Canada
Boars	New Hebrides
Butter	Norway
Cigarettes	Prisoner-of-war camps and in post-war Europe
Cocoa beans	Mexico
Cowries (shells)	World-wide (South Sea Islands, Africa, America, and Ancient Britain)
Fish hooks	Gilbert Islands
Fur of flying fox	New Caledonia
Fur of black marmot	Russia
Grain	India
Hoes and throwing knives	Congo
Iron bars	France
Knives	China
Rats (edible)	Easter Island
Salt	Nigeria
Shells	Solomon Islands, Thailand, New Britain, Paraguay
Skins	Alaska, Canada, Mongolia, Russia, Scandinavia
Stones	South Sea Islands
Tobacco	Virginia
Whale teeth	Fiji (used for the purchase of a bride or a canoe)

Using cattle or oxen in exchange for other goods (as did the Hebrews and Greeks and, later, the Masai tribe of Kenya) was still a cumbrous system. Traders took time to make a settlement, if they reached agreement at all. The quality of the animals varied. So did the quality of the goods for which they were exchanged. Cattle and oxen, when used as money, were portable and recognizable, but not durable, divisible, or homogeneous.

The next step in the development of money therefore came about when the trading countries round the Mediterranean and Aegean seas began to use metals for exchange purposes. The metals were gold, silver, and copper: precious enough to be wanted, useful and decorative enough to be generally acceptable, and their quality did not vary with time. Probably the earliest people to use metal as money were the Assyrians of Cappádocia, whose embossed silver ingots date back to 2100 B.C. The Assyrians may even have had a primitive banking system including what we now call 'interest': payment for loans and debts.

By the eleventh century B.C., bars of gold and electrum were traded between merchants. Electrum is a naturally occurring mixture of gold and silver which was 'panned' from the rivers of Lydia and Phrygia (now south-west Turkey) by the same methods the gold seekers tried in 1849 during the Californian gold rush: washing the dirt from the river bed until only gold remains.

The bars or lumps of electrum were not coins, for they were of differing weights and quite plain, but they had great advantages over the exchange of goods by barter and over the use of animals as a form of money. Metals do not rot or perish, so deferred payments could be arranged. But there were disadvantages, still.

Metal bars were bulky. They did not easily pass from hand to hand. They were difficult to divide. The quality and quantity of the metal in different bars was not the same. The ratio of gold and silver in electrum varied. Traders in different parts of the world often used different weights, so metal bars had to be balanced against one another (in other words, weighed) before goods could be exchanged.

30

In the book of Genesis, Chapter 23, occur the lines:

> 'I will give thee money for the field. Take it of me and I will bury my dead there. And Ephron answered him ... the land is worth 400 shekels of silver.... And Abraham weighed to Ephron the silver, which he had named in the audience of the sons of Heth, 400 shekels of silver, current money with the merchant.'

Because of the need to weigh metals to ensure that they were of the correct value, as Abraham did in the above episode, traders tried to identify their own metal bars by marking them. Smaller pieces of metal, easily handled, were later produced, and marked in the same way as the large pieces had been, so that they, too, would be recognizable by traders.

It was hard at first to decide how much metal should be exchanged for cattle. Eventually the amount of gold, silver, or copper was made equal to the local value of an ox. This measure was called by the Greeks a *talanton* or 'talent'. A copper talent weighed 60 lb.

The Babylonians used shekels for their weights: 60 shekels equalled one manah, and 60 manahs equalled one biltu, which was the average weight of a Greek copper talent. When Sir Henry Layard excavated a site at Nineveh in 1845 he found a series of bronze and stone weights which showed these calculations. The weights can be seen today in the Assyrian collection of the British Museum in London.

The process of marking small pieces of metal was probably how the first coins were produced in 700 B.C., when the Lydians of Asia Minor gave their electrum pieces the head of a lion on one side and nail marks on the other.

From Lydia the use of coins like these spread to other areas such as Aegina, and the states of Athens and Corinth; to Cyrenaica, Persia, and Macedon. China, Japan, and India were also using coinage about this time.

By about 400 B.C. beautiful coins were being minted by the Greek-speaking peoples around the Mediterranean. An interesting one from Cnossus in Crete shows on one side the god Zeus and on the other side the labyrinth from the legend of Theseus and the Minotaur.

The story goes that Daedalus, a Greek architect, made the labyrinth or maze for King Minos of Crete. In the labyrinth, which was so tortuous that no one could escape from it, lived the Minotaur—a savage creature with a man's body and a bull's head. Theseus, son of the King of Athens, decided to kill the Minotaur, so he joined a party of luckless Greek youths and maidens who were to be sacrificed to the Minotaur. But Ariadne, the daughter of King Minos, fell in love with Theseus and gave him a sword to kill the monster and a ball of thread to guide him back to the mouth of the labyrinth. According to the legend, Theseus did indeed slay the Minotaur, and with the aid of Ariadne's thread escaped from the maze.

Daedalus, the architect of the labyrinth, who himself was imprisoned there because of his past misdeeds, escaped from Crete with his son Icarus by using home-made wings attached to their ankles by wax. But Icarus flew too near the sun, the wax melted, his wings fell off, and he plunged to his death in the sea below.

Most Greek coins were like this one from Cnossus, showing a god on one side and a tale from their many wonderful myths on the back. The coins circulated widely. Those from Macedon, which had the richest gold mines in Europe, were used in all the known world during the reign of Alexander the Great, and were even copied by British tribes. One such coin, a 'stater', was unearthed in Hampshire at the Danebury excavations in 1969. The size of a sixpence, but twice as thick, it dates from the first century B.C. The horse, which figures on early Macedonian coins as a horse and chariot, grew less distinct as it became copied in Europe. On this Danebury coin, however, it is clearly recognizable.

Alexander went on many military campaigns. By 324 B.C. he had reached Kabul, and gone through the Khyber Pass to northern India. Here he defeated the army of Rajah Porus and a force

[British Museum.

Historical Greek Coins.

1. Philip II of Macedon.
2. Alexander the Great.
3. Lysimachus of Thrace.
4. Seleucus I of Syria.

5. Ptolemy I of Egypt.
6. Demetrius Poliorcetes of Macedon.
7. Mithradates the Great.

of 200 elephants. A silver coin portraying elephants in battle was struck to depict this event.

But Alexander's end was near. He died the next year. His portrait was then stamped on a silver coin. He thus became the first person to have his likeness on a coin. One of Alexander's generals, Lysimachus, King of Thrace, arranged the issue. But another general, Ptolemy, was not so respectful. He seized power in Egypt, founded a new dynasty, and put his own portrait on coins. Furthermore, he became the first living ruler to do so.

5

CASH: COINS

THE COINS AND BANK-NOTES in your pocket are described as 'ready money' or 'liquid money', since, unlike money deposited in a bank, they are available for spending immediately. Another term for them is 'cash', from the French word *caisse* meaning a money-box or chest.

Nearly all the cash circulating in the world today is (apart from paper money, discussed in Chapter 6) made up of *token* coins. A token coin is one whose metal content is less than the face value. In other words, it is worth more as a coin than it would be if melted down for scrap. A *standard* coin, on the other hand, is one where the value of the metal is equal to the face value stamped on the coin. Most early coins began as standard, and thus a silver penny contained exactly one pennyworth of silver.

But even coins which began as standard could come to a bad end. Unscrupulous kings rubbed off metal from the edge of gold coins, or put quantities of lead into silver coins to gain money to finance wars. In Henry VIII's time the coins issued in 1544 contained one-seventh less silver than those issued in 1543; Henry continued in this way until, by the time coins were issued in 1551, they contained only one-seventh of the original amount of silver.

The idea of a standard coin was that it should be a coin of guaranteed weight and purity of metal. It would therefore have a

Officers receiving and weighing coin at the Exchequer. A.D. 1130 (*circa*). From a manuscript in Trinity College, Cambridge.

value of its own, quite apart from being a measure of the value of other things. The Jewish shekel was first a weight of metal, then a coin.

To get a definite standard, something had to be chosen that varied only within narrow limits. Henry III used a grain of wheat

From an illustration in Diderot's *Encyclopaedia*, 1763, which shows the minting of coins. Several workmen are engaged in different occupations. One at (*a*) is casting, another at (*b*) is striking coins, and another at (*c*) is melting gold in the furnace. The workshop is provided with anvils (*d*), shears (*e*), workbenches for striking coins (*f*), and a table (*g*) for trueing-up the pieces.

(a)

(b)

|Coins Weekly.

Siege Pieces. (a) Ormonde Shilling, (b) Cartwheel
Penny.

from the middle of the ear, 24 equalling one pennyweight of
silver: so a silver penny had to weigh the same as 24 grains of
wheat. Twenty pennyweights equalled 1 ounce, and 12 ounces
(240 pennyweights) weighed one Troy pound. Henry VIII
introduced the 'avoirdupois' pound for weighing butchers' meat in
the market, and this measure gradually came to be used for coarse
goods of all kinds, while the lighter Troy pound was used by
jewellers and apothecaries (early chemists). Though the pound has
equalled a variety of different coins in different ages, its original

British Museum.

Queen Anne's Touchpiece given to Doctor Johnson. (Note the pierced hole so that the coin could be worn.)

meaning was a pound weight of silver. Mark and livre were also originally weight terms. But in times of stress, and also because of royal and imperial waste, standard coins were often 'debased' and their value changed to something less.

In early days the kings of England had their standard coins

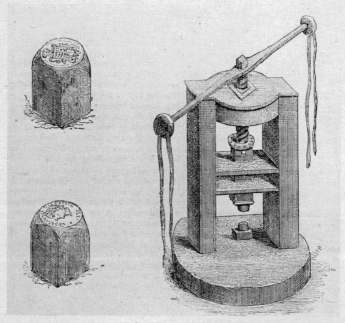

Radio Times Hulton Picture Library.

Press and dies formerly used in the Royal Mint at the time of George II.

[Central Office of Information.

The new Royal Mint at Llantrisant, Glamorgan, South Wales, which was opened by Her Majesty The Queen in December 1968. After heat treatment in an annealing furnace, coin blanks drop on to a conveyor which takes the blanks up and discharges them into inspection hoppers.

minted in monasteries. Such places, it was thought, would be free from theft. From the thirteenth to the seventeenth centuries gold and silver were made into long bars. These were then cut into pieces of exact weight for sovereigns, angels, crowns, and shillings. Then a design would be stamped on them with a hammer to make the pieces perfect money.

39

Today the Royal Mint at Tower Hill in London produces medals and coins for Britain and sixty-seven countries overseas, while the Llantrisant Mint in Glamorgan produces Britain's decimal coins; but because of limited space at Tower Hill it is expected that all minting will eventually be transferred to the new buildings at Llantrisant.

Countries Supplied with Coinage by the Royal Mint from 1954 Onwards

Australia	Gibraltar	Nigeria
Bahamas	Greece	Panama
Bahrain	Guernsey	Paraguay
Bhutan	Guinea	Peru
Bermuda	Guyana	Philippines
British Caribbean	Hong Kong	Qatar and Dubai
Territories	Iceland	Rhodesia and Nyasaland
British Honduras	Iraq	Seychelles
Brunei	Isle of Man	Sierra Leone
Burma	Jamaica	Singapore
Ceylon	Jersey	S. Arabian Federation
Colombia	Jordan	Somalia
Congo	Kenya	Tanzania
Costa Rica	Kuwait	Tonga
Cyprus	Lebanon	Trinidad and Tobago
Dominican Republic	Libya	Uganda
Ecuador	Malawi	Uruguay
Eire	Malaysia	Venezuela
El Salvador	Maldive Islands	Vietnam
Ethiopia	Mauritius	West Africa
Fiji	Muscat	Western Samoa
Gambia	New Zealand	Zambia
Ghana	Nicaragua	

Into the Mint come 56-lb. ingots of copper from South Africa, Canada, and Zambia. Nickel from Canada arrives in 5-cwt. drums. Tin ingots come from Cornwall; zinc plates from Poland, Bulgaria, and other east-European countries. Silver bars, from North and South America, the Soviet Union, and South Africa, are made into medals.

United Kingdom coins from 5p upwards are made from cupro-nickel, an alloy of 75 per cent copper with 25 per cent nickel. The

| Central Office of Information.

The picture shows a general view of a line of coining presses. Each press produces 200–250 coins a minute.

$\frac{1}{2}$p, 1p, and 2p are made from coining bronze, an alloy of 97 per cent copper with $2\frac{1}{2}$ per cent zinc and $\frac{1}{2}$ per cent tin.

The metal to be used is heated in 850-lb. batches for about 70 minutes in a furnace (some are electric, others are oil-fired), and the molten alloy is poured into cast-iron moulds dressed with oil to prevent sticking. The bars of metal taken from the moulds are rolled into strips between several pairs of rollers. Because the rolling process hardens the metal, the strips have to be softened, or annealed, by being passed through another furnace at 700° C. Then a second rolling process is applied to bring the strips to exactly the thickness specified for the particular coin being produced.

Blank discs are stamped out from the strips, and after being washed and dried each blank has its rim raised to protect the coin's face and to allow for easy stacking. They are now placed on a moving belt, and an examiner picks out any that are defective. The blanks are fed by a hopper, or moving container, on to an instrument called a 'die', which bears the reverse impression of the pictures to go on the coin. As each blank drops on to the bottom die (the 'head' or 'obverse' die), it is held steady by a collar

|Central Office of Information.

Electronic counting and bagging machines in the Royal Mint at Llantrisant.

while the top die squeezes down—with a pressure of 250 tons for large coins—and the process is repeated 250 times a minute.

The newly struck coins are again examined for defects, and the satisfactory pieces are counted or 'told' on machines, including electronic tellers (which are replacing older types) at a rate of 17 coins a second. These machines count the number required to fill a 50-lb. bag and automatically switch off.

[Keystone Press.

The Trial of the Pyx.

All the bags are weighed, but those weighing most and least are rechecked. If they hold the right number of coins the bags in between must also have the right number. Other weight checks are made throughout all processes, and again before the coins leave the Mint.

The last test of the coins is a very important one. Two are taken from each bag: one goes to be tested by the Assay Department within the Mint, the other goes into a box called the *pyx* kept at the Royal Mint specially to hold specimen coins awaiting examination at the annual *Trial of the Pyx*. The keys of the pyx were originally held by a Warden, Master, and Comptroller, who met at the royal command, opened the box, and submitted the coins to a jury of goldsmiths. They weighed and tested the coins, and if an error was found, the mint workers faced terrible punishments. They might be condemned as traitors, mutilated, fined, or exiled.

The Trial of the Pyx goes back 600 years to the reign of Edward III. It continues annually today—though without the savage penalties, of course. An independent jury of goldsmiths meeting at Goldsmiths' Hall are charged by the Lord Chamberlain to declare if the coins in the pyx deviate in any way from the required standards of purity and composition. An unfavourable verdict would mean the return of the coins and a new issue to take their place. A favourable verdict publicly affirms the standard purity of the coins.

Though the Trial of the Pyx is not carried out publicly, and there has never been an unfavourable verdict, it is not just a ceremony but an actual test of the purity and composition of the coins issued by the Royal Mint.

6

CASH: PAPER MONEY

COINS, LIKE THE ANCIENT specimens mentioned at the end of Chapter 4, or the much later varieties described elsewhere in this book, possessed all the qualities that good money must have: they were acceptable, homogeneous, divisible, portable, fairly stable in value, yet durable. Why, then, has it been necessary to introduce paper notes which do not last very long, and whose content, unlike gold or silver coins, has no value at all?

One reason is that large amounts of coin are very bulky. Imagine having to pay a £5 bill in pennies. And what about £50, £500, or £5,000 bills? Such large masses of coin passing back and forth would make trade very inconvenient. Indeed, people might even claim danger money for handling such obvious masses of money, which are a temptation to thieves.

The second reason for the introduction of paper money was that coins could not be produced in sufficient amounts for the vastly increased world trade that developed from the seventeenth century onwards. Thirdly, that same increase of trade meant that there were more profitable uses for metal than as exchange pieces.

Finally, there was the danger of loss or robbery. Carrying large amounts of valuables or quantities of metal about one's person could be a tiring and useless exercise. There was the ever-present

The first printed note for £5, made payable to Abraham Newland, Chief Cashier of the Bank of England (1793).

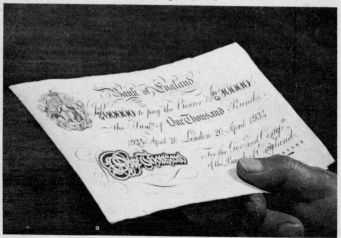

The highest United Kingdom denomination note—for £1,000.

risk of robbery by highwaymen; and delicate bargaining might be hampered by the sight of a gold bar sticking out from a trader's pocket. One of the arguments for the cheques, credit cards, and giro systems used today is that such systems reduce the amount of cash in transit, and therefore reduce theft.

In earlier times men who for one reason or another did not want to carry valuables about with them, left them in the safe keeping of a silversmith or goldsmith and got a receipt. This receipt could be used to pay debts to the value of the gold or coin deposited with the smith. Gradually the receipt, which unlike gold or silver had no real value of its own, became itself acceptable in payment of debt, at least among the people who could read.

As these receipts were for a certain indivisible amount, notes began to be issued by the goldsmiths so that, for example, instead of giving out a receipt for £10, he would give out two receipts for £5 each. Each receipt promised to pay the bearer £5, so that these receipts or *notes* could be used for two transactions for £5 each instead of only one for £10. Gradually notes came to be issued for uneven amounts like £10 13*s*. 6*d*.

Money in the Making—the final plate is curved ready for the printing of the notes.

In the seventeenth century the task of issuing notes was taken over by the bankers, and so the bank-notes we know today were finally introduced.

As we saw in Chapter 1, money that is made acceptable by law is called legal tender. In the United Kingdom the Bank of England has the sole right to issue legal-tender paper money, which it does in the form of bank-notes. Scottish notes, though acceptable in

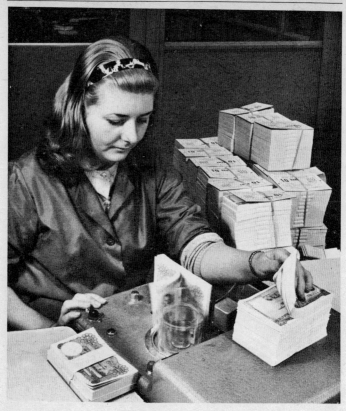

Counting notes by machine.

Scotland and sometimes abroad, are not legal tender, but they are backed by a corresponding Bank of England issue. In 1969 the Royal Bank of Scotland discovered £250,000 worth of its five-pound notes had been forged, so it called them all in and reprinted the whole note range. All new issues are very beautiful. (£1 illustrated on page 50.)

In most countries today paper money is issued by a central or national bank acting on behalf of the Government. But in time of crisis another body may do so. In the United Kingdom, for example, during the First World War and for a short time after-wards, the Treasury, instead of the Bank of England, issued notes. They were called 'Bradburys' after John Bradbury, who signed them. In the American Civil War the cotton planters of the southern states often issued their own notes.

Convertible paper money is money that can be exchanged on demand for gold, as was the case in England up to 1914. Paper money that cannot be so exchanged is known as *inconvertible paper*. British bank-notes and those of most other countries today are inconvertible paper.

Early paper money had to be convertible, because people were not willing to accept as money anything which had no value. Gold was valuable in itself and therefore acceptable. Paper was not. But convertible paper gave a claim to gold, and so it gradually became as acceptable in payment or in exchange as gold itself.

The amount of convertible paper that could be issued was limited by the amount of gold available, because any note could be exchanged for the same value in gold (thus a £1 note could be changed for a gold sovereign). This limitation on the amount of paper money that could be issued guarded against 'inflation', which means more and more money being needed to pay for fewer and fewer goods.

But convertible paper has disadvantages, too. In a developing country there is an increase in the number of goods and services produced. If the issue of paper notes remains the same because of a static amount of gold this alters the prices of the increased amount of goods. Thus if we start with 100 saucepans and £100 the pans will cost £1 each. If 200 saucepans are now produced, and the amount of money, £100, remains the same, the pans will cost only 50p each. The price of the goods is half what it was before (which is the same as saying the value of the £1 has doubled, for it buys twice what it did before). When values or prices change in a country this creates hardships for buyers or sellers of goods. One of the disadvantages of convertible paper money is therefore that the supply or issue of notes is related to the amount of gold held by the issuing authorities, and not to the supply of goods.

Another disadvantage of convertible money is that prices may depend not on what is actually happening in one's own country

[*The Royal Bank of Scotland.*

The Royal Bank of Scotland, front and back of green £1 note, with (front) view of Forth
Bridge, and railway bridge in background, and watermark at front lower right.

but on what is happening in other countries. Britain may be
sending gold out of the country to pay for imports (goods sold to
Britain by countries abroad) and as a result has less gold. This
means that Britain must issue fewer notes. Britain therefore now
has more goods (her own plus the imports) and less money. As we
saw in the previous paragraph, less money and more goods means
lower prices. This is another disadvantage of convertible paper
money: a Government cannot control its country's prices without
taking into account what is going on in other parts of the world.

Inconvertible paper means that the number of notes issued does
not depend on the amount of gold available. Any number of notes
can, in theory, be issued. This is a big temptation to unscrupulous
or inefficient Governments. If too much paper money is issued for

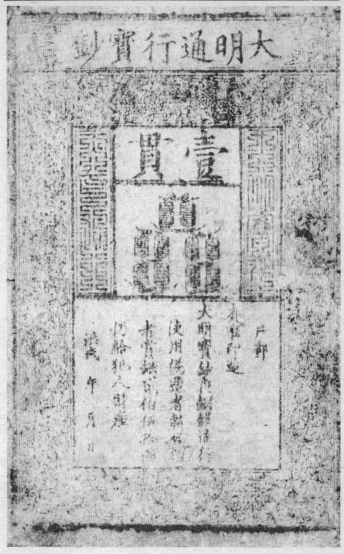

[The Institute of Bankers Collection of Paper Money.

The Precious Notes of The Great Ming (Chinese), 1375. One of the oldest surviving examples of paper money.

the amount of goods produced in the country there will be too much money chasing too few goods. The prices of the goods will go up. Imagine £100 available in a country for 100 saucepans. The pans will sell at £1 each. But if more money, e.g. £200, is available for the same 100 saucepans they will sell at £2 each. The prices of goods have doubled. So has the amount of money. (This is another way of saying the value of money has fallen, for £1 buys half of what it did before.) A lot of notes will have to be given in exchange for what cost only a few notes before. Also, foreign countries will offer less of their currency for the 'inflated' notes. In 1923 Germans who wanted to buy foreign currency had to give billions of marks for a single dollar or pound sterling.

Wars or other crises help to debase a country's currency. Precious-metal coins are filed down, made more impure, or give way to token coins. Inconvertible paper money takes the place of gold. This is why part of a country's history can be learnt from a study of its currency.

The earliest paper money is thought to date from the T'ang dynasty of China in the seventh century A.D. The oldest surviving notes belong to the Ming dynasty (1368–1644) of China and are made of mulberry bark. Described by Marco Polo, they were circulating before the discovery of America and can still be found in good condition in dealers' shops today.

The 100 'cash' note of the Great Ming, which can be seen in London in the Institute of Bankers' collection of paper money, was first issued in 1375, together with six other denominations. A thousand 'cash' or copper pieces equalled 1 kwan (one string), at that time worth one ounce of silver. The 'string' was an actual piece of string on which 1,000 copper 'cash' could be threaded. This explains why Chinese coins had a hole in the centre.

Stockholm was the first town in Europe to issue bank-notes. Johan Palmstruch set up a bank in Stockholm in 1656, and four years later issued notes to replace the heavy copper coinage then circulating (see page 13). The 100-daler note with Palmstruch's signature and seal, is now very rare.

Notes can have a face value for any amount. There are high

[H. R. Harmer, Ltd.

Stamps of countries with high inflation, showing over-printing, and postage stamps used as money.

Top row: Showing three countries (China; Germany; Danzig) which had high inflation.

Second row: Russian stamp used as currency. First two stamps show back and front. Inscription says: 'Having circulation on par with copper money.' Other two are the same but inscription reads: 'Having circulation on par with silver subsidiary coins.'

Third row: Shows an Italian stamp used as a coin in circular frame. Reverse reads: 'Banca Dell'Italia Meridionale.'

Bottom row: Shows front and back of Rhodesian currency cards of 1900.

denominations like the rare nineteenth-century American $10,000 notes, of which 1,000 are thought to be in circulation. By contrast, there is the small-change paper money or *Notgeld* issued in Germany during and after the First World War when silver coins were hoarded because they had a metal content greater than their face value. The city of Strasbourg alone kept 6 million marks in small change in its city vaults.

Small denomination notes for 3, 5, 10, 15, 25, and 50 cents were also put out during the American Civil War when coin was similarly scarce. The early ones were perforated and called 'postage currency'. They cost today about £1·50, but some of the rarer types bring in as much as $1,000 at auction sales.

Postage stamps have been used for currency in small amounts. The 1915 Russian 10-, 16-, and 20-kopeck issue, for example, served as either postage stamps or money. In 1900 in Rhodesia stamps mounted on cards measuring 3 inches × 2 inches were used as money.

Some note issues, like the *assignats* of the French Revolution, were turned out in such vast quantities that many are still quite cheaply available as collectors' items even though some of them are 150 years old.

China is a country which has had a very large note issue. During the troubled times of Chiang Kai Chek communist and nationalist parties continually issued their own notes in areas they occupied. None of the notes was backed by gold, silver, or other metal, and the continued fighting did not create confidence in either party's note issue. Inflation on a scale like that of Germany in the 1920s took place. After the Second World War Chinese 1- and 5-yuan notes had to be replaced by denominations of up to 250,000 yuan. But the world's worst inflation occurred in Hungary in 1946, where the paper pengos were so worthless that 130 *trillion* of them equalled one gold pengo of the 1931 issue.

Paraguay's first paper money, printed in 1865, is still very common today—like the notes of the Chinese civil-war period mentioned above, but for a different reason. Shortly after the notes were issued Paraguay became involved in a war with her South American neighbours and was almost annihilated. The people died, but the paper money lived on: there was nobody left to spend it.

During the Second World War the manager of a plantation on

Fanning Island in the Pacific had an emergency issue of notes printed for the use of his employees and the U.S. and New Zealand troops occupying the island. About 1,000 green £1 notes went into circulation, inscribed: 'Fanning Island Plantations Ltd., Fanning Island. One £ Pound Australian Currency. Redeemable only at the office of the Company at Fanning Island.' When the notes were withdrawn after the war most of them were cut up and used as admission tickets for the local cinema. The 360 or so remaining intact are much sought after by collectors.

Notes have been issued in an astonishing variety of shapes and sizes, ranging from the tiny one-cent Bank of Taiwan note (less than 3 inches by $1\frac{1}{2}$ inches) to the huge notes of fourteenth-century China (13 inches by 9 inches) and Tsarist Russia. Denominations range from the £100 Bank of Scotland to the Hong Kong notes for a fraction of a penny.

The important thing to remember is that any bank-note can be classed as paper money, no matter what its face value, no matter what size or colour of paper it is printed on, *provided it is immediately acceptable in payment of debt.*

What about cheques, postal orders, and credit cards—are these also a form of paper money? The answer is that they are not money, but *claims to money.* Because such paper is nearly but not quite money, it is often referred to as *near money.*

'The Banker and his wife': a painting by the Flemish artist, Quentin Matsys (c. 1460–1530).

7

BANK MONEY

AS WE HAVE SEEN, GOLDSMITHS' notes (receipts for valuables deposited) were the first form of paper money in England. Though not legal tender, they soon became acceptable between traders in payment of debt. At one time merchants used to deposit cash and valuables in the Tower of London. When Charles I seized £120,000 of this in 1640 the merchants got it back only after much protest and long delay, so they naturally grew more cautious about where they left their money. From that time onwards merchants placed their gold for safe keeping in the vaults of trusted goldsmiths.

The goldsmiths, who were astute business-men, soon realized that they need not hold all the money deposited with them all the time. Not every merchant or nobleman was going to present a receipt for repayment of his goods at the same minute, or even in the same week. Months and even years might pass before a creditor came to ask for his valuables back.

Goldsmiths therefore began a practice still used today, known as **fractional-reserve banking.** This meant keeping only a proportion of the deposits, and investing the rest. Fractional-reserve banking depends upon careful handling of the fraction of deposits kept as cash in reserve. Many goldsmiths and early nineteenth-century banks failed because they issued notes for more money or

|The Times.

The largest cheque ever issued: £119,595,645 12s. 0d. drawn by Lazard Bros. in favour of the National Provincial Bank, 24 January 1961, in connection with the take-over of the British Ford Motor Company.

valuables than they possessed, or ever would possess, and because they did not ensure that in time of need they had enough cash reserves ('liquid' money) to meet all demands.

Even in the early years of the present century, over 6,000 American banks failed because they could not immediately pay back deposits on demand. Today there are stringent safeguards in the leading banks against failure.

The most successful of early goldsmiths knew from experience what was the greatest amount of money that would be asked for at any one time, and they kept this amount lying ready in their vaults and safes. They then used the rest of the money in more profitable ways: buying ships or cargoes and selling them at a profit; lending to other customers who paid them 'interest' for the use of the original money.

The payment of interest for the use of money had been frowned upon by the early Christian Church. They thought it sinful to charge a man anything for lending him money. This meant that non-Christians, particularly Jews, for whom the practice of charging interest was not a sin, became skilled in money matters, especially as many other professions were closed to them.

Radio Times Hulton Picture Library.

One way to save your money.

We see this in Shakespeare's *The Merchant of Venice.* The Jew, Shylock, lends money to Antonio's friend, Bassanio, Antonio providing his ships on the high seas as security. Shylock, in revenge for Antonio's past cruelty to him, asks for a pound of Antonio's flesh in payment if Antonio's ships do not arrive by the date promised. And they don't. Must Antonio now pay the pound of flesh? Portia, the heroine, fortunately finds a clever legal answer. Shylock may have his pound of flesh, but if he takes any blood, which is not mentioned in the bargain, his life will be forfeit.

Some Christians soon began to rival those outside the Church in the lending of money. They would lend it for a short period free, but if the debt was not paid back at the time promised the Church's laws allowed the delay to be charged for. By making the free period very short and the delay charge very high, the money-lenders were *just* keeping within the laws. Moreover, if some end product was involved, or the risk of loss shared by a group, a charge for the use of money became acceptable. A group of men

A Chubb Treasury Door. This strongroom door can have an overall thickness of 24 in. and weigh over 20 tons. Each of the four combination locks is capable of 100,000,000 changes of code. This door also has a time-lock device. You can set the clock to a certain time, and even if the combination code is correctly carried out, the door still will not open until the chosen time.

could therefore act as goldsmiths or money-lenders quite legitimately.

In the Middle Ages crusaders needing ready money for their expeditions to the Holy Land would pledge their estates with the goldsmiths in return for a loan. Later, traders or farmers needed money for raw materials. With time and labour, the finished goods became worth much more. It was as profitable, therefore, for goldsmiths to lend money in the early stages of these ventures as it was for traders generally to borrow it. A great increase in trade in the sixteenth and seventeenth centuries resulted from this lending and borrowing.

An even greater increase in the borrowing of funds came about in the eighteenth century with the beginning of the Industrial Revolution, for the canals and machinery introduced at that time needed money to bring them to fruition—just as a space programme or motorway does today. Goldsmiths, rich landowners, and prosperous merchants pioneered modern banking by lending to inventors and industrialists.

The English banking system today is made up of three parts. First, there are the Commercial Banks, also called Joint-Stock Banks: these are the banks (Barclays, Lloyds, Midland, etc.) which deal with the general public through their branches in the High Street. The present chapter is concerned with the working of these banks. Secondly, there are the Merchant Banks and Discount Houses, which deal only with special customers and selected trading ventures. Finally, there is the Bank of England, described in Chapter 8, which acts as the Government's banker.

The practice of fractional-reserve banking, introduced by the goldsmiths, means that a bank does not keep all the money entrusted to it idle in a till or vault. Suppose one man deposits £1,000 in a bank account and is prepared to leave the money there for a month or two? In a deposit account (or, as the Americans call it, a 'time account') he will be paid interest for doing so. If a deposit of £1,000 brings £50 payment for a year the interest rate is 5 per cent (£5 per year on each £100 deposited).

Why do the banks pay this money; this interest? Simply because the banks know that, like goldsmiths of an earlier generation, they can use the £1,000 deposit, or at least part of it, profitably. The banks can get 10 per cent interest, or more, by lending it to someone else—to somebody with new business ideas, to somebody building a new machine, or making a new product.

But suppose the depositor of the £1,000 suddenly wanted his money back? A bank would certainly be in an awkward position if it had only one customer, only one deposit, and was working entirely on its own. But a bank has many depositors entrusting their money to its care, and each bank is usually part of a large organization with many branches. This means that each bank can always pay a customer without delay because funds can be sent from one bank in the same organization to another which may be having exceptionally heavy withdrawals.

Banks do not lend out *all* the money deposited with them. They keep part in cash in their counter tills, and part in their own deposit account at the Bank of England. These two amounts, in the till and at the Bank of England, are both reckoned by the banks as 'cash' and amount to 8 per cent of their total deposits. This 8 per cent is known as the **cash ratio.**

The other 92 per cent is made use of in various ways. About 25 per cent (the minimum is 20 per cent) is lent on very short-term loans to Discount Houses and to the Government against the security of Bills of Exchange or Treasury Bills. These 'bills' are claims to money in the future in return for the loan of immediate money, discounted at a fair rate of interest. For example, a Treasury Bill for £10,000 guarantees that the Government will repay £10,000 in 91 days' time (three months) in return for borrowing less than £10,000 now. The actual amount borrowed varies from week to week with the supply of, and demand for, money. Suppose the agreed price was £9,800. This is a discount of £200 over the three months. The bank or Discount House lending £9,800 for three months will receive £10,000 when the 'bill' falls due for payment. This discount is its profit, or interest, on the loan. The chief point to note about these very short-term loans is that the bank is entitled to reclaim the money almost immediately. Money 'at call or short notice' is repayable either at once (call) or within three to seven days (short notice). The banks regard this cash as available to meet any sudden rush for money

[Barclays Bank Ltd.

Inside a bank today: Barclays Bank, the High Street, Doncaster branch.

by depositors, as happens when wars or rumours of wars start a financial panic. This extra reserve, with the cash ratio, is called the **liquidity ratio.** Ratio simply means fraction.

The rest of the 92 per cent, let us say 70 per cent, is kept in the tills and used as the cash ratio for a very much larger set of loans to businessmen who wish to expand their enterprises. It is this part of bank activities that many people find difficult to understand.

Let us suppose that a depositor, Dan, pays £1,000 into the bank, as a deposit. Later in the same day, another customer, Bob, comes to see the bank manager. He is about to produce a new type of boat, which he thinks will prove profitable. Unfortunately Bob is short of money to buy materials and equipment needed for this venture. He proposes to buy these things for £2,000 from Boat Provisions Ltd., a firm of wholesalers in the trade, provided the bank manager will make him a loan. Of course the bank has only £1,000, and it must keep some of this as cash ratio, and some more for liquidity ratio, but the bank manager is confident everything will be all right if Bob can put up some security. Bob has no very safe security to provide, except a life-assurance policy. This will only provide a small sum if surrendered, but a large sum if Bob dies. The bank manager agrees to accept it, as **collateral security.** This means security *lying alongside* a debt.

Let us now look at the bank's Balance Sheet.

COMMERCIAL BANK OF NEWTOWN LTD.			
Liabilities (*owed by the bank*)		*Assets* (*owned by the bank*)	
	£		£
Deposit by Dan	1,000	Cash (cash ratio)	240
Deposit by Boat Provisions Ltd. (who fortunately bank with Commercial Bank Ltd.)	2,000	Debts owing by Discount Houses (the rest of the Liquidity Ratio at call)	760
		Debt by Bob	2,000
	£3,000		£3,000

Notice that the original £1,000 has grown into £3,000. In other words, the bank has *created money*. Why is the bank manager confident that everything will be all right? Because he knows that depositors rarely ask for their money back straight away. Boat Provisions Ltd. may not ask for their money for months and months. In the meantime Bob will be selling his boats and paying back the money with interest.

President Roosevelt, one of the greatest of American presidents, once said at a time of serious unemployment: 'All we need is confidence.' If bank managers are prepared to create money in this way businesses can go ahead to the benefit of the whole country. Notice that Bob's £2,000-worth of materials and machinery did not even require the use of money at all. The cash did not even leave the bank. Bob's cheques were honoured and entered in the wholesaler's account without the cash ratio having to leave the till. Of course if Boat Provisions Ltd. had banked with any bank other than Commercial Bank Ltd. the latter would have been in difficulties. But as *all* banks are creating money in this way, there would probably have been someone else who did bank with Commercial Bank Ltd. making a cheque deposit to even the matter up. At any rate, the bank manager was confident that this would be the case.

The simple story of Bob and Dan serves to illustrate the tremendous importance of money deposited in the banks. In fact, bank money makes up the greater part by far of Britain's wealth. In June 1968 the grand total of money in Britain was £14,634 million, of which £10,975 million was in bank deposits. The remainder, which we call cash or 'liquid money', consisted of £280 million in coins and £3,379 million in paper money (£3,220 million in Bank of England notes, £148 million in Scottish bank-notes, and £11 million in Northern Ireland bank-notes).

How much of their deposits the banks are allowed to lend, even to whom they are allowed to lend, is not a hit-or-miss affair. The proportion of deposits kept in actual cash (either in the till or at the Bank of England) is 8 per cent, as mentioned already. Another 22 per cent of deposits is kept in what is called 'near-money' (investments which can be turned back into cash almost immediately, if necessary). So $8 + 22 = 30$ per cent of deposits are in either cash or near-money.

When the Government wants to make people spend less, and borrow less, the banks have to raise their liquidity ratio. In other words, they must keep as cash or near-money some of the funds they would otherwise have lent to customers such as Bob. As a result, Bob would be unable to produce his boats, and the general public would thus be prevented from buying Bob's boats and other luxuries.

The banks are therefore very unusual and powerful concerns: their lending increases the amount of money in the country. But they are not quite as important as they once were, for they are no longer the only institutions who lend money. Nowadays building societies make loans to house purchasers, finance houses lend money for hire-purchase transactions, and insurance companies also have funds available for borrowers. Like the banks, these bodies also create purchasing power when they lend money.

The New Fetter Lane Branch of Barclays Bank.

Banks and other money-lending institutions must keep a careful watch on the ratio of loans to deposits. The more liquid cash they hold, the less profitable their business becomes. The less liquid cash they hold, the greater is the risk that they may not be able to repay their depositors on demand.

[*The Mansell Collection.*

'England's Curse.' An angry history of the National Debt from Henry VI to William IV.
(1832.)

8

THE BANK OF ENGLAND

AT THE BEGINNING OF THE previous chapter we saw how the money-lending activities of the goldsmiths and early bankers grew to keep pace with the expansion of trade and industry in the sixteenth and seventeenth centuries. But there was no established means by which the Government could borrow. A rich man might be glad to finance some trading venture, yet he was usually reluctant to lend his money to the Government or to the King for the purpose of fighting wars.

William III's accession to the English throne in 1689 meant that England became involved in the war which William, as ruler of Holland, was fighting in alliance with almost all Europe against Louis XIV of France. Money was needed for this costly war (sometimes called the War of the English Succession, because Louis XIV supported James II's claim to the English throne against that of William III), which lasted from 1689 to 1697. Ireland understandably did not want to finance a war against the Catholic King Louis, and the English showed very little enthusiasm either.

Against this background, in 1694, a Scotsman, William Paterson, thought of a scheme which would remedy the shortage of Government cash and suit both lenders and borrowers. A

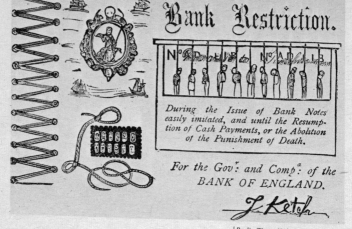

George Cruikshank's celebrated 'One Pound Note' of 1819, a comment on Peel's stringent measures to protect the paper currency. It provoked so much agitation that no forger was afterwards hanged.

group of businessmen would set up a bank to lend money to the Government. To do this they needed permission from the Government, since the Monopolies Act, 1624, allowed monopoly or exclusive company trading rights only by a Charter of Incorporation, granted for a limited number of years.

The businessmen therefore lent £1,200,000 at 8 per cent interest plus £4,000 a year expenses in return for a Charter, later renewed in exchange for further loans. The lenders of the money were guaranteed their interest by duties on the tonnages of ships and the sale of beer, ale, and other drinks. The Tonnage Act was passed for this purpose. So the Government's bank, the **Bank of England** came into being.

The Bank of England issued notes or receipts for the amount lent, and the first receipts were written by hand on paper which the Bank bought from a nearby stationer. The stationer's sales shot up as other people bought his paper and tried to forge Bank of England notes. But the Bank soon realized what was happening, and in future used specially made paper for its notes.

As well as carrying interest, the notes could be cashed for the whole or part of their face value. When a man presented a £10 note and only wanted £9 cash, the amount received by him would be written on the note, which he kept. He could then present the note later with the £9 endorsement on it, and he would get the final £1 owing. The note then became the property of the Bank.

One note was presented to the Bank of England in the early twentieth century for all but one penny of its face value, so that the bearer of the note could keep it as a souvenir.

The notes or receipts issued by the Bank of England were always intended to be *convertible*, in other words, they could be exchanged freely for gold. Gold had been deposited (as a loan) with the Bank, so it was expected that gold would be repaid on presentation of the receipt. However, so great was the expense of fighting the so-called War of the English Succession that only a year after the Bank opened its doors it shut them again—at least for the purpose of exchanging paper for gold. It did not resume this business until 1698, after the war was over.

|Radio Times Hulton Picture Library.

The Bank of England, showing the Accountant's Bank Note Office in the 1880s.

While the Bank of England had begun borrowing on a grand scale, goldsmiths continued to issue their own notes. But in 1708 the Bank Charter Act forbade groups of more than six people 'to borrow, owe or take up any sum or sums of money on their bills or notes payable at demand or at any less time than six months from the borrowing thereof'. This meant goldsmiths and private banks became partnerships or very small family businesses, except in Scotland, where the Act did not apply.

A further restriction was imposed by the 'Bubble Act' of 1720, which was designed to prevent any recurrence of the South Sea Bubble disaster. The disaster happened like this: the South Sea Company had, in exchange for certain concessions, offered to take over the National Debt (money owed by the Government, and on which the nation had to pay interest). The Government agreed, and the Company issued £100 shares. These, bought with more enthusiasm than sense, rose to £1,000. Speculation grew, and when the paper shares later proved worthless thousands of people were ruined.

The 'Bubble Act' resulted in the Bank of England obtaining a Royal Charter and a monopoly of London banking business for well over a century.

Bank of England notes were not at first legal tender, i.e. a payment a debtor can legally compel his creditor to accept. People did often accept the notes, but they had the right to demand coin instead. So much gold left the country to pay for the American War of Independence (1775–83), the wars with revolutionary France, and the Napoleonic War, that insufficient gold remained for bank-notes to be exchanged on demand for coin. In 1797 the Bank Restriction Act was therefore passed to make Bank of England notes legal tender for any amount. War with the French ended briefly in 1802, began again in 1803, and lasted till 1815. Six years later there was enough gold in the Bank of England to make its bank-notes convertible, so they again ceased to be legal tender until 1833. From that time to 1914 they circulated with, and were exchangeable for, gold. By that time too, almost every country had gone on to the 'gold standard' (see Chapter 10).

Meanwhile in 1844 an important Bill had been passed—the Bank Charter Act. The issue of notes by small banks or goldsmiths had been far from satisfactory. Not all of them had the high standard of honesty and efficiency expected of banks today.

[*Radio Times Hulton Picture Library.*

The Bank of England: the Bank Note Store Office of 1870.

Some people in Parliament even blamed the financial troubles of the country on the habit of banks and goldsmiths of issuing too many notes.

So in 1844 came the beginning of the present system, by which the Bank of England has the sole right to issue legal-tender notes

73

[*The Bank of England.*

The Bank of England today.

in Britain. The Bank Charter Act meant that no new bank setting up could issue notes at all. If existing banks joined with others, or went bankrupt, they lost their right to issue notes, and the Bank of England took over two-thirds of their previous note issue itself. Finally, all banks were limited in their note-issuing powers. They could never issue more than the average they had turned out in the twelve weeks prior to the passing of the 1844 Act.

The effect of the Act was gradually to make the Bank of England all-important in the supply of notes. The Act also introduced a **fiduciary issue** of notes: 'fiduciary' comes from the Latin word *fides* meaning faith, and a fiduciary issue is one where the notes are not backed by gold but by some other promise to pay.

If paper notes are convertible it is essential that enough gold coins are available for everyone who wants to change paper notes into coin. But ensuring that for every piece of paper printed there is a gold equivalent means having a lot of gold. It means, too, that the amount of notes and what they can buy is related to the amount of gold.

The fiduciary system introduced in 1844 therefore allowed £14 million of the country's note issue to be backed not by gold but by Government bonds or securities. A fiduciary system is used by most countries today, though the percentage of gold backing varies.

The size of the fiduciary issue is no longer as important as it was originally. In fact, an official report on the workings of the British monetary system has pointed out that 'the authorities do not regard the supply of bank-notes as being the only, nor nowadays the only important supply of money, and the Government's function in issuing notes is simply the passive one of ensuring that sufficient notes are available for the practical convenience of the public'.

The chief function of the Bank of England is, and always has been, to act as bankers to the British Government. This does not mean that the Bank lends money directly to the Government (except on a small scale overnight). It *does* keep all the accounts necessary to keep track of payments by the different ministries and government departments. The most important of these is the Exchequer Account, which finally receives all tax payments to the Government and pays all disbursements by the Government for contracts and activities on behalf of the nation. If the Government needs money it can either sell stocks (on which it pays a fixed rate of interest) or it can issue *Treasury Bills* through the Bank.

Treasury Bills are issued in certain multiples of £5,000, and last for three months. If the Government offers a Treasury Bill with a promise to pay the bearer the sum of, say, £10,000 in three months' time the would-be purchaser knows he must wait three months for the bill to be worth £10,000. So he certainly won't offer £10,000 for it today. But if it were on sale to him today at £9,850 he might buy it. He wouldn't mind waiting three months to cash the bill, for in that time his £9,850 would have earned him £150, which works out to be an interest of about 6 per cent per year.

The Treasury Bill market is described as 'an open market by

tender', which means that anyone wishing to buy the Bills can make an offer. The chief buyers are Discount Houses—specialized banks who make a profit out of *bill-broking*. Bill-broking is the business of borrowing money on short-term loans and lending it out at a higher rate than that at which it was borrowed. Profit margins are small, and the brokers must be experts. The Discount Houses make the Bills of Exchange and Treasury Bills up into convenient dated batches, each batch being cashable on a different day. Banks find these Bills a very satisfactory source of interest-bearing near-money—a profitable yet 'liquid' asset. The cash they pay for them is loaned by the Discount Houses to finance home and foreign trade.

The Treasury Bill, invented in 1877 by Walter Bagehot, provides the Government with a useful weapon for controlling the country's spending. When the Government wants to boost the economy the Bank of England *buys back* Treasury Bills from the Discount Houses. This means that the Discount Houses have more money to lend to other borrowers: trade expands and more employment will result. On the other hand, if the Government *sells* more Bills it is taking money away from the Discount Houses, and that money is no longer available for industrial investment. Hence the economy is 'squeezed'.

The Bank also helps control the economy in other ways. It uses **Bank Rate** as a particularly powerful weapon to control the level of business activity. Bank Rate is the rate at which the Bank of England will discount *first-class Bills of Exchange*. A first-class bill is one that is absolutely reliable, so that the payer will be certain to pay on the due date. When lending money, bill brokers naturally charge more for bills that are risky, or unreliable. Bank Rate is charged on the very best bills, and more than Bank Rate on the riskier ones. Since people borrowing money for their businesses hope to make a profit, the raising of Bank Rate discourages them from expanding. The money will cost more to borrow, so all projects will be less profitable. Lowering Bank Rate will make money cheaper, and business more profitable. If the

[*Midland Bank Ltd.*

A fish-eye view of the Midland Bank's computer.

Bank of England lowers Bank Rate businessmen will be encouraged to go ahead.

Another control the Bank can use is the system known as **special deposits.** The ordinary commercial banks have accounts at the Bank of England, which they regard as part of their cash ratios. Suppose some (say 2 per cent) of these deposits were 'frozen' by the Bank, so that they could not be used if a financial scare caused heavy withdrawals by the public. This would be a serious blow to the cash ratios of the commercial banks. It would stop them loaning money so freely. Creating money would be more risky, and the banks would reduce their lending activities.

The last activity which the Bank of England performs on behalf of the Money Market is the **Bankers' Clearing House System.** Since all banks have accounts with the Bank of England, the simple way to clear any debts between them is to transfer the money from one Bank of England account to the other. First let us see why banks get in debt to one another. The two examples below will help to explain.

CHART I: MR. A. AND MR. B
(both bank at Barclays Bank)

MR. A (who has £1,000 in Barclays)		MR. B (who has £500 in Barclays)
pays Mr. B £100		pays the cheque into his account
Opening Position: £1,000	+	£500 = £1,500
Closing Position: £900	+	£600 = £1,500

At the end of the transaction Barclays position has not changed, so we see that when people use the same bank no clearing problems arise.

CHART II: MR. A AND MR. B

MR. A (who has £1,000 in Barclays)	MR. B (who has £500 in Lloyds)
pays Mr. B £100	pays the cheque into Lloyds
Opening Position: Barclays £1,000	Lloyds £500
Closing Position: Barclays £900	Lloyds £600

At the end of the transaction Barclays must give Lloyds £100.

Imagine this happening with millions of cheques every single day. At the end of the day, with several banks involved, a clearing process must take place. Using the Big Four Banks as examples, we have, at the end of an imaginary day:

SUMMARY OF CLEARING (£ million)

Name of Bank	Amount owing to others	Amount due from others	Net indebtedness to other banks
Barclays	46	48	−2
Lloyds	36	32	4
Midland	51	53	−2
National Westminster	45	45	0

Notice that the National Westminster group came out all square on the day, as the value of cheques demanding payment exactly equalled the value of cheques received. Lloyds owe £4 million; half of it to Midland and half of it to Barclays. The passing of credit-transfer slips of these amounts will clear up the entire affair. Cheques worth £178 million have been cleared in a few seconds at the Bank of England.

A Lottery advertisement of 1777.

9

WHERE MONEY GOES

WHERE DOES MONEY GO? IT goes round and round, and as it circulates it helps in the production, distribution, and exchange of 'real' wealth. By 'real' wealth we mean the goods and services that we all need to keep us alive, well, and happy. How does this money system really work? A simple description has to be given in stages.

Stage 1: Money Earned for Producing 'Real' Wealth

The goods that we need have to be grown in the fields, forests, and grasslands of the world, or made in the factories and workshops. This production cannot take place without the effort and willing co-operation of men and women of every sort: engineers, chemists, welders, carpenters, machinists, assemblers, packers, truck drivers, tractor drivers, labourers, and so on. The reward that mankind is going to receive from all this activity is a flood of goods and services, but the reward that each employee will receive will be some money. Just how much money a particular employee will earn depends upon his skill and knowledge, or upon the output he has achieved.

Why do we pay the employee in money? Why not give him some of the goods he has produced? As already explained in Chapter 1, employees do not wish to be paid in watches, if they are watchmakers, or in flour if they are millers. Because we produce by specialization, with each factory concentrating on one type of commodity, the owner of the factory is unable to offer a balanced share of the world's goods. It is better to give the employees money wages, so that they may purchase in the shops a balanced diet, and an assortment of useful goods.

Stage 2: Money Spent on Consuming the Goods Produced

This purchase of the goods and services needed is the second stage of the money system. Now the people who have been specializing in their particular part of the production process have a day off from work to go out on a shopping spree. They buy with their money the things that appeal to them. Shall it be a new 'pop' record, or a toy for the baby, furniture and carpets, or fruit and wine? There will certainly be some necessities, like food and clothing; there may be luxuries once in a while. Something must be set aside to pay for services like gas and water, electricity and the telephone, rent and hire payments for television or radio. Something must be set aside for possible future use, perhaps for holidays, or hospital treatment, for times of sorrow or gladness. These savings will probably not be hoarded, as they would have been in olden times. We no longer sew our savings up in the mattress of the bed, or bury them in the garden in a stone pot as our ancestors did. Today we invest them in the banks, insurance companies, and building societies. The activities of these firms are the next stage in the money system.

Stage 3: Money Invested for Future Prosperity

Banks and similar firms have a great part to play in the money system. First they are useful intermediaries in the ordinary activities of stages 1 and 2 above. They help employers pay wages and salaries by supplying them with notes and coins in the right sizes and quantities. They help the employees by opening an 'account' for anyone who wishes to leave his money in the bank and only take out some of it for everyday use. They arrange payment of debts through the cheque and credit-transfer systems.

[*Radio Times Hulton Picture Library.*

'Your money or your life.' Stagecoach passengers are robbed by highwaymen.

The second type of function the banks and similar institutions perform is not concerned with day-to-day activity but with long-term activities called **investments.** Investments enable firms to redesign factories and plant with the latest machinery and equipment. If production is to be kept to a high level we must constantly replace our capital assets like buildings, machinery, and tools. Money is needed to buy these things, and it is our savings in the banks that make it possible. The banks lend the funds we leave with them (being careful to keep some cash available for anyone who requires some). These loans to businessmen, or to the Government, keep our whole country 'in good heart', with new factories, shops, and offices, schools, colleges, and hospitals, roads, railways, and harbours.

One of the most famous of these institutions is the **Stock Exchange.** The Stock Exchange is a market where those who wish to 'invest' in a firm or industry can buy the shares of that firm or industry from those who prefer to withdraw their investment and have cash instead. Suppose an investor (we will call him Smith)

'The Tax upon Property.' Drawing by George Cruikshank.

[Radio Times Hulton Picture Library.

The Underwriting Room at Lloyds about 1886.

puts money into the Mogul Oil Company Ltd. Mogul will use his money to build a refinery, or a mammoth tanker, or to drill a well in the North Sea, or the Arabian Gulf. They cannot give him back his money, for they have spent it. If he wishes to regain his money—perhaps because he has lost his job and is in need of funds—Smith must sell the shares on the Stock Exchange. In order to do so he phones his stockbroker.

'Hallo, Mr. Jones. Smith calling. I wonder if you could sell my 500 Mogul shares for me. The truth is I've lost my job.'

'I'm very sorry to hear that, Mr. Smith. The market is pretty strong today. You should get a fair price. I'll go over to the House at once and ask around the oil market.'

Mr. Jones hurries over to the 'House' in Throgmorton Street, and asks several of the oil jobbers (a jobber is a dealer in shares) what prices they have in Mogul shares today.

One says £2·521/2·534. Another says £2·525/2·540.

In each case the lower price is the price the jobber will buy at. As Mr. Jones is selling Mogul shares, the price of £2·525 is the better offer. (Notice that dealings go down to tenths of a penny.) Mr. Jones clinches the deal at £2·525 each for 500 shares.

'Hallo, Mr. Smith. I've managed to get you a very good price.

|Radio Times Hulton Picture Library.

The Stock Exchange in the nineteenth century.

500 sold at £2·525. Will you post me the Share Certificates? And I will let you have a cheque shortly. I do hope you'll soon find work again. Good afternoon, and thank you.'

Like all *highly organized markets*, the Stock Exchange is a most efficient organization. Over £1,260 realized on the sale of Mr. Smith's shares in a few minutes, and with as little fuss as you or I would make to buy a bar of chocolate or a packet of cigarettes.

Stage 4: Money Management—the Government's Part

Sometimes people, and even firms, get nervous and depressed about the future. When they do this they tend to be cautious in their spending policies, because they fear bad times will soon

|The Stock Exchange.

The Stock Exchange today.

come. This leads to a smaller demand for goods and services, and unemployment grows. A 'depression' sets in, and a 'depression' grows into a 'slump'. This is a time when unemployment is widespread, the money system has broken down, and general gloom prevails.

At other times people, and firms, get supremely confident. They buy and buy and buy. Firms expand output, build new plant, dig new mines, or buy new cars and lorries. There is no unemployment now. Everyone is working, earning good money, enjoying a fair share of the world's goods. 'Boom' times have come, and everyone is cheerful, until prices begin to creep up higher and higher and inflation is upon us. Inflation is when too much money is chasing too few goods. People earning good wages find they cannot afford the necessities of life. It is as bad as a slump, but not quite so depressing.

This is the last stage of the money system. When we suffer from either of these economic illnesses—a depression or an inflation—the Government steps in to control the money system. Only a Government can manipulate the money system to solve these difficult problems. If people are buying too little, so that a depression sets in, the Government starts to spend instead. A

Government always has useful things that need to be done. Roads can be widened and improved; schools and colleges can be built; swimming pools and recreation grounds are needed all over the country. Even unemployment benefit and family allowances can be used to raise the spending of the people. Once the money begins to go round again the economy will soon recover.

If people are buying and borrowing too much the Government will start a 'credit squeeze'. It raises interest rates so that borrowing costs more, and puts legal restrictions on the sums borrowed. It puts taxes on goods to make them dearer and not so tempting to buy. It sells shares (or stock) at tempting prices, so people use their bank cash to buy those securities. This lowers the banks' deposits, and therefore the amount they can lend. The Government may tell the banks not to lend so much, and to whom to lend. It has more direct methods too. It can freeze wages, dividends, and prices, so that they do not rise.

The result of these measures is that the inflation in the economy will be reduced. People will work harder and raise output, and as money gets scarcer with the 'squeeze' there will not be too much money chasing after too few goods.

This is the way the money system works in an advanced country. Without our knowing it, goods have been brought from the far ends of the earth to satisfy our needs. The prospect of earning money—either as wages, rent, interest, or profit—has made the resources of the whole world and the skills of mankind available to all of us.

10

GOLD AND INTERNATIONAL MONEY

GOLD IS A REMARKABLE metal. One ounce of it can be beaten out until it extends over a surface area of 100 square feet. Gold can be drawn into a wire so fine that 544 feet weigh about one gramme. It is pleasant to touch, easy to count, will not rust or spoil, and is highly decorative.

In space, on earth, and under the sea, gold is wanted. Undersea cables on the sea bed must operate faultlessly, and so the circuitry of repeater units in these cables is made of gold, efficient and imperishable.

America's space probes used gold. In the moon project, gold coatings protected the electronics systems from the blast of rocket motors and the heat encountered on re-entering the earth's atmosphere. Because gold is an imperishable non-tarnishing conductor, it is also used for the circuitry of the computers that guide the moon flights.

In aircraft such as the V.C.10, the windscreen is made of a sandwich of laminated glass containing a transparent film of gold. This film, less than two-ten-millionths of an inch thick, is electrically heated to prevent icing, misting, and dazzle; it also helps to filter out the harmful rays of the sun. The Rolls-Royce engines of the Concorde were plated with gold to control the heat generated.

Buildings, too, can be gold-plated. Such decoration costs

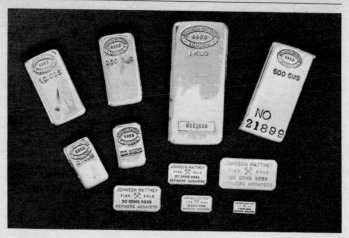

|Johnson, Matthey & Co. Ltd.

A selection of small gold bars produced for trading, investment, and gift purposes.

around 30p a square foot. The Fox and Hounds Inn in Los Angeles has a conical roof made of gold ceramic tiles that never tarnish, but are washed regularly with toilet soap.

Throughout the ages gold has been used for adornment, and even today the main use of gold is in jewellery. But it also performs important monetary functions. It is the base on which are built comparative exchange rates for most of the world's currencies; gold settles balance-of-payments differences. Two per cent of subscriptions to the World Bank, set up at Bretton Woods in 1944 to help developing countries, are paid in gold, and so are one-quarter of the quotas to the International Monetary Fund. Many people zealously hoard gold. It is estimated that between 1965 and 1969, 600 tons of non-fabricated gold went into France, and a further 100–200 tons to private domestic hoarders of bullion in Germany, Switzerland, and Italy. Ranks of the gold hoarders increase whenever there is a monetary crisis.

Gold coins circulate no more. Once famous pieces like the Louis d'or, the double eagle, the Napoleon, the Belgian gold franc, or the English sovereign are no longer used as exchange pieces. Probably the only domestic coin left is the Mexican 50 pesos.

Almost all other gold coins, e.g. the Austrian ducat, the British sovereign, or the South African Kruger rand are minted only for foreign sale. Historically, however, gold coins often reveal a country's commercial importance and its pattern of trade.

When Roger II, Duke of Sicily, struck gold coins in the twelfth century (with his Latin title, *Dux Apuliae*, which some people think gave the name ducat to later coins) he ended the supremacy of the silver coinage, which had lasted for five centuries.

The great commercial cities of Italy in the thirteenth century issued the gold florin weighing about one-ninth of an ounce, with a lily on the obverse; and the ducat with a standing figure of Christ, and the Doge of Venice and St. Mark. The ducat, used in Holland, Austria, the Netherlands, and Denmark, afterwards became known as the sequin or zecchino.

Louis IX (1226–70) instituted a gold coinage for France, and from that time there were many issues of gold coins. In the fourteenth century Louis of Bavaria introduced a gold florin into Germany, a similar coin being issued in the next three centuries by numerous rulers, cities, and bishops. The florin was also established in Austria and Hungary.

Spain made a large issue of gold coins from her possessions in the New World, the first bearing impressions of Ferdinand and Isabella of Spain. They are still common.

In the seventeenth and eighteenth centuries Spanish doubloons (from the Spanish word *doblon*, meaning double) and Portuguese dobras made the wealth of the American colonies known all over the world.

King Offa of Mercia had struck a gold dinar in the eighth century, and Henry III had experimented with gold coinage in the thirteenth century, but it was Edward III who began the first regular issue of gold coins in England. Edward's gold 'noble' introduced in 1351 weighed just under half an ounce and was valued at 6s. 8d. The obverse showed the King in a ship.

Edward IV added a rose to the ship; the coin was then known as a 'rose noble' or 'ryal', and the value was raised to ten shillings. A new gold coin to replace the noble at 6s. 8d. was the gold

[*B. A. Seaby, Ltd.*]

Some Famous Trading Coins

		Present Value £
1. Philip III, 359–336 B.C. gold stater.		185
2. Athens: silver tetradrachm 186–147 B.C.		35
3. Julius Caesar: silver denarius.		90
4. Hadrian, A.D. 117–138: copper sestertius.		—
5. Byzantine Empire: Isaac II, 1185–95: gold scyphate nomisma.		45
6. Ancient British (S.E. England) tin money, probably made from Cornish tin.		30

'angel', so called from the obverse side showing St. Michael over-throwing Lucifer. The angel became the coin given to those who had the disease of scrofula, which it was thought could be healed by the king's touch. Such coins became known as touchpieces.

During the reign of Charles I (1625–49), the angel ceased to be issued as currency, but small copies of it, touchpieces, were made for later Stuarts down to Henry, Cardinal York, in the eighteenth century, the last person to claim the healing power. A touchpiece given by Queen Anne to Dr. Johnson can be seen in the British Museum.

Henry VII (1485–1509), the first of the Tudors, issued a large coin weighing over half an ounce, and also the first shilling. Henry

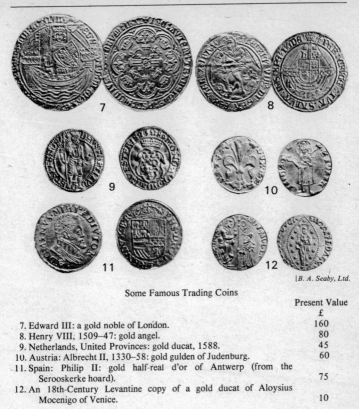

Some Famous Trading Coins

	Present Value £
7. Edward III: a gold noble of London.	160
8. Henry VIII, 1509–47: gold angel.	80
9. Netherlands, United Provinces: gold ducat, 1588.	45
10. Austria: Albrecht II, 1330–58: gold gulden of Judenburg.	60
11. Spain: Philip II: gold half-real d'or of Antwerp (from the Serooskerke hoard).	75
12. An 18th-Century Levantine copy of a gold ducat of Aloysius Mocenigo of Venice.	10

VIII introduced a gold crown of five shillings copied from the French *écu*. Until the time of the Stuart kings, when the gold crown was replaced by one of silver, Wales and Cornwall supplied gold to the Royal Mint, where it was mixed with foreign gold.

In Scotland the gold mines produced sufficient of the metal for James V to issue ducats made entirely of Scottish gold.

After the union of Scotland and England (1603) a gold 'unite' was issued with a value of 20s. This was replaced in 1619 by the 'laurel'. A thistle crown (worth 4s.) and half-crown were also struck in gold. Guineas appeared in four denominations after the accession of Charles II, but not as a regular issue. Pistrucci's sovereign came in 1816, and its disappearance in 1917 ended a

Some Famous Trading Coins

[B. A. Seaby, Ltd.

Present Value
£

13. Spain: Charles III: silver 8 reals, 1772 from Lima (Peru) mint, countermarked with Chinese character as having been used in the Orient.   50

14. Spain: Charles IV: gold 8 escudos, 1802, Madrid mint. These are commonly known as 'doubloons'.   50

15. Austria: twentieth-century restrike of the silver thaler of 1780: still made for trading in Ethiopia and parts of the Middle East.   2

coin that had been used in one form or another for nearly 400 years.

The prestige of the French *écu* in the sixteenth century caused it to be widely copied throughout Europe. At the end of the seventeenth century the *Louis d'or* was similarly important, and led to Italy, France, Belgium, and Switzerland adopting a gold decimal currency standard when the Latin Monetary Union was formed in the middle of the nineteenth century. These countries were joined later by the Scandinavian countries, but not by Britain which had a 22-carat sovereign. The 1914–18 war hindered further monetary co-operation.

In 1871 Germany's currency was simplified and a 20-mark gold piece, similar to the English sovereign, became the unit of the

[B. A. Seaby, Ltd.

Some Famous Trading Coins

	Present Value	
	£	s.
16. British Trade Dollar, 1911.	2	
17. India: gold one mohur (East India Company), 1882.	30	
18. Austria: Franz Joseph gold 4 ducats of 1915. The illustration is of a recently made official restrike.	12	10

German-speaking nations. Discoveries of gold in South Africa, Australia, and California led to a great increase in the gold coinage of the world, especially in the United States.

Since the Middle Ages the coinage of the East has been mainly of silver. The Mogul Empire in India in the seventeenth and eighteenth centuries, however, had a considerable issue of gold *mohurs*. When Nadir Shah sacked Delhi, the wealth he carried off enabled him to break the monopoly of the silver currency of central Asia by an issue of gold. But the only gold currency of importance in the East was that of the Emirs of Bukhara used in central Asia in the nineteenth century.

An issue struck in Berlin for South Africa during the presidency of Kruger is interesting as it has an error. The coins for 20s. and 10s. showed on the reverse side a wagon with two shafts, instead of one.

Worse still, the designer, Otto Schultz, gave further offence by

95

putting his initials O.S. on the edge of the president's portrait. The letters were too small to be seen except by a close scrutiny, but Kruger thought they were an insult, for 'os' in Dutch means ox. The coins, naturally enough, were soon withdrawn.

Gold coins are minted today mainly for commemorative issues or for export sale. Belgium absorbs large quantities of new gold coins, including around five tons of new sovereigns a year. Though officially minted, these are not legal tender and are bought mainly by coin collectors.

Under a full **gold standard,** gold coins as well as bullion are used to pay for goods and services both at home and abroad. Gold flows freely from buyers to sellers. The value of any currency is fixed at a certain weight of gold of a certain fineness. When Britain was on the gold standard, the Bank of England was obliged by law to buy gold at £3·8875 per *standard* ounce, i.e. gold eleven-twelfths fine.

If all currencies are fixed to a certain definite weight of gold, they are linked to one another in the same way. At one time the pound sterling was worth four times as much gold as the American dollar. Therefore $4 = £1. Now suppose the demand for dollars is strong, because many countries wish to buy American goods, while the demand for pounds sterling is weak, because few people want to buy British goods. The dollar will begin to rise in value, from $4 = £1 to $3·90 = £1. (As the dollar gets more valuable you need less of them to buy £1.) It may be that it will pay a merchant not to buy dollars at all, but to change his £1 into gold at the Bank of England and ship the gold. When the dollar gets so dear that it is cheaper to ship gold, gold will move out of a country that is on the gold standard.

When a country loses gold it must take steps to regain it again. For one reason, the note issue is tied to the gold stock. If we lose gold we shall have to call in notes. To recover the gold, Bank Rate is raised. This attracts foreign gold into the country, since it can earn high interest rates. It also makes business less profitable and leads to unemployment. This lowers the demand for foreign goods and weakens the currency of foreign countries, while it makes home goods cheaper and better value for money, so that foreigners are more willing to buy. This strengthens home currency, and gold begins to flow back in. The gold standard is therefore a self-correcting mechanism which operates through the deflation or inflation of the economy.

There are a number of reasons why this system is not used today. The chief of them is that nations, Britain, for example, do not want to suffer mass unemployment every few years in order to keep the *balance of payments* right.

So in 1944 a new system was set up. The price of dollars was fixed to gold: 35 dollars an ounce. Other countries were linked with the dollar, and thus indirectly to gold. The £ sterling in 1970 was worth 2·40 dollars, and therefore $2 \cdot 40 \times \frac{1}{35}$ ounces of gold.

Suppose that I, living in Britain, wish to buy something from America. I need American money. I offer my £1 to a bank and ask for dollars in exchange. But the bank can only exchange my £1 if they have dollars. They will have dollars only if previous traders who have sold to the United States have handed in their dollars in exchange for pounds. If there have been no sales to (or gifts from) the United States there will be no dollars. Traders wanting to buy American goods will either not be able to or will have to borrow dollars or something else equally acceptable: perhaps gold. This borrowing has to be paid back by earning more dollars; i.e. selling more goods to people who possess dollars.

The Bank of England tries to save gold and foreign currencies like dollars or marks or francs for the time when British traders want, say, dollars in exchange for their sterling. The account where the Bank saves gold and foreign currencies is called the *Exchange Equalization Account.* Because of the varying demand for sterling, the rate of exchange can move quite safely between the limits of £1 = $2·38 and £1 = $2·42 (i.e. about 1 per cent on each side of the $2·40 average). But when everybody wants to sell sterling, so that it is in danger of falling below the $2·38 'floor', the Bank of England buys sterling with the dollars or other currencies it has saved from the good days. This buying sends the rate for sterling up again. (When someone is buying, the price usually goes up.) The account is used to 'equal out' the buying and selling of sterling, and this is why it is called the Exchange Equalization Account.

But if Britain persistently sells less, year after year, to America than the Americans sell to Britain, then more dollars will go out from the Bank's pool of foreign currencies. Gold, equally acceptable, will go out too. This situation is called a 'balance-of-payments deficit'.

Suppose that a country has no more gold or foreign currencies left to pay for goods its inhabitants need from abroad. It cannot offer more pound notes (or whatever its currency happens to be) for less dollars, because the exchange rate is fixed around $2·40 to £1. If a deficit continues, the rate may be fixed lower down. This movement is then known as **devaluation.** If, for example, the rate went down from £1 = $2·40 to £1 = $2·00, this would be a devaluation of sterling. It would cost British traders more to buy American goods. When they gave up their pound note they would get only two dollars for it instead of $2·40. Why devalue, then? Because British goods become cheaper for Americans to buy; in this way it is hoped to attract dollars into the country. They will build up into a stock-pile, eventually to be used by British traders to buy American goods.

We have used American dollars to illustrate the balance-of-payments situation, but any currency will do. Countries trade all over the world, and build up debit and credit balances with other nations all the time. Temporary shortages can be overcome by borrowing, but if there are debits year after year a country must devalue.

A country can borrow foreign currency from the *International Monetary Fund.* When this was set up at Bretton Woods in the United States in 1944, each member country pooled a proportion of its currency plus 25 per cent gold into a common fund. They borrow from it when they need foreign currencies, but they cannot do so indefinitely. The danger is that some currencies may be wanted all the time, and others not at all.

It is thought today that the International Monetary Fund has an insufficient pool of gold and foreign currencies, and it should provide paper claims, like bank cheques, instead. This would help world trade, which cannot work without money. The scheme is known as Special Drawing Rights, or Paper Gold, and the details are still being worked out.

But countries are gradually learning that what harms one, harms all, what benefits one, ultimately benefits all—or as John Donne put it:

'No man is an Island, entire of itself . . .

Any man's death diminishes me, because I am involved in Mankind; and therefore never send to know for whom the bell tolls; it tolls for thee.'

11

DECIMAL CURRENCY IN BRITAIN

FROM 15 FEBRUARY 1971, THE date chosen for Britain to begin a decimal currency, 95 per cent of the world has been counting their money in tens.

Altering a currency is one of the most important changes a country can make. It affects everybody who uses money, from the smallest child just getting his first pocket money to the oldest person receiving a State pension over the Post Office counter. It concerns the makers and users of calculating machines, the writers and publishers of textbooks: in Britain, 5 million machines needed to be replaced or converted, and 2,000 books needed revising.

There must be good reasons for making such a tremendous change. In school the time and energy spent in learning two sets of rules, one for 'ordinary' arithmetic in tens, and one for 'money' arithmetic in twelves and twenties, will be lessened, perhaps more than halved. Other subjects or interests can be taught in the saved time.

Shoppers and shop assistants will find calculations easier and quicker to make. Credit and finance transactions of all kinds will be more simple and less prone to error.

Business machines are used all over the world, and £ s. d. machines have to be specially altered for a small and dwindling

The new Halfpenny Piece. The reverse design shows the Royal Crown and is the work of Mr. Christopher Ironside, who also was responsible for the reverse designs of the other five decimal coins.

market. Changing to decimal machines will eventually mean a saving in costs and a wider choice of machines. The decimal system chosen by Britain is much better for computer use than the old £ *s. d.* It will make for easier programmes, faster running time, and take up less space in the computer's memory, thus speeding up all kinds of calculations and reducing their costs.

In Britain the changeover has been harder than in most other countries because the scale is larger. The number of business machines affected was ten times that in Australia, though the population is only four times as large. But the resultant speed, ease, and accuracy of calculations and the time saved in schools and business has more than compensated for any early difficulties. The cost of the changeover, the Institute of Management declared, was won back within a year.

Australia and New Zealand found that within only a few months of changing their currency to the decimal system greater accuracy and speed was obtained in all calculations; errors were more easily located; handling cash was easier and faster; and migrants and tourists found the new system simpler to understand than the old.

Let us take a look at Britain's decimal coins, the bronze ½p, 1p, and 2p, and the cupro-nickel 5p, 10p, and 50p. Each new penny is worth 2·4 old pennies, for, instead of £1 equalling 240

|Central Office of Information.

The 1 New Penny Piece. The reverse design
shows a portcullis with chains royally crowned,
being a badge of King Henry VII.

pennies as in the old system of coinage, £1 now equals 100
pennies.

The £1, £5, and £10 notes remain. The ten-shilling note, first
introduced in 1914, has been replaced by the 50p piece, the only
seven-sided coin in the world.

The equilateral-curve heptagon of the 50p coin is sometimes
called a Reuleaux polygon because the mathematician Reuleaux
described the shape in his book, *The Kinematics of Machinery*
(1876). An equilateral-curve heptagon has the unusual qualities of
constant breadth and being able to roll easily. This means that a
coin like the new 50p is a useful one for slot machines. Furthermore, not being a round coin, it can be easily distinguished from
other coins in a purse, wallet, or till, as well as by blind people.

The 50p replaced the ten-shilling note for reasons of economy:
though a coin is initially dearer to produce, it should last for fifty
years, whereas the average life of the old note was only five
months.

The £ symbol and the decimal point must appear together; the
£ symbol and the p sign never together, so that it is correct to
have:

58p		£0·58		£0·58p
33p	OR	£0·33	BUT NOT	£0·33p
½p		£0·00½		£0·00½p

|Central Office of Information.

The 2 New Pence Piece. The reverse design shows the badge of the Prince of Wales: three ostrich feathers enfiling a coronet of crosses patté and fleurs-de-lis with the motto '*Ich Dien*'.

Why not £0·005 instead of £0·00½? The answer is that there are 100 units of new pence in the £, not 1,000 units. Therefore, except in calculating machines, the ½ symbol is the one to be used, not a third place of decimals.

Why introduce the ½p at all? To have 1p as the smallest unit would mean no near equivalent of the old £ *s. d.* penny, and the value of the smallest new coin (equal to 2·4 old pence) would be too high. Decimal currency is designed to last. If the value of the smallest coin were 1p or 2·4 old pence, to drop this coin (like the old farthing) because of falling values would leave 2p as the smallest coin. The result would be a shortage of small change and much hardship. If it ever became necessary to drop the ½p, however, this would leave 1p as the lowest coin in the system, so the basic structure would be unimpaired. The United States, the first country to adopt a decimal currency, used ½ cents in 1782, and so did France when she went over to decimals in 1783.

How many new coins were needed? By the summer of 1969, eighteen months before D-day, the new Royal Mint at Llantrisant in Wales had produced 1,000 million decimal 'copper' coins. For 150 years British coins were made at the Royal Mint, just outside the Tower of London. But lack of space there meant that the production of all the new decimal coins as well as coins for

Central Office of Information.

The 5 New Pence Piece. The reverse design is the badge of Scotland: a thistle royally crowned.

countries overseas, would have to be undertaken somewhere else. Llantrisant, in Glamorgan, was the place chosen. There they had both the space and machinery to produce the 4,150 million coins which were required for Decimal Day.

SHOPPERS' CONVERSION TABLE (from £ s. d. to £p)		
£ s. d.	£p	
1d.	$\frac{1}{2}$p	+ 0·2d.
2d.	1p	+ 0·4d.
3d.	1p	− 0·6d.
4d.	1$\frac{1}{2}$p	− 0·4d.
5d.	2p	− 0·2d.
6d.	2$\frac{1}{2}$p	Exactly equal
7d.	3p	+ 0·2d.
8d.	3$\frac{1}{2}$p	+ 0·4d.
9d.	4p	+ 0·6d.
10d.	4p	− 0·4d.
11d.	4$\frac{1}{2}$p	− 0·2d.
1s.	5p	Exactly equal

Only 6d. and multiples of 6d. convert exactly into decimal currency. But the table above means that the same number of prices are rounded up as down, and buyers' and sellers' gains cancel out.

An interesting feature of the old £ s. d. 'silver' coins was their weight/value relationship, a florin weighing four times as much as

|Central Office of Information.

The 10 New Pence Piece. The reverse design is part of the crest of England: a lion passant royally crowned.

|Central Office of Information.

This is the obverse design common to all six denominations of the new decimal coinage. It is the work of Mr. Arnold Machin, O.B.E., R.A.

a sixpence, and twice as much as a shilling, while a half-crown weighed five times as much as a sixpence. This weight/value relationship dates back to the time when coins contained their face value in precious metals.

A weight/value relationship has been kept in the new decimal coins not for historical reasons but because such a relationship makes it possible for those people who handle coins in bulk to check the total value by weighing instead of counting. The 10p cupro-nickel coin is twice the weight and value of the 5p. The 2p coin is twice the weight of the 1p and four times the weight of the $\frac{1}{2}$p.

|*Central Office of Information.*

The 50 New Pence Piece. This is the sixth coin of the decimal series, and was first introduced for use in place of 10s. notes in October 1969. The reverse design is a new version of Britannia.

The 50p is not in weight/value relationship to the other cupro-nickel coins, because if it were it would have to be an excessively large and clumsy coin. If a 20p coin is later introduced it will be related to the weight and value of the 50p. It will also have the same shape, so that the two largest coins can be quickly sorted from the others, and then weighed to calculate their total value.

The idea of a decimal currency first appeared in a pamphlet of 1586 by a Dutch mathematician, Simon Stevin. He declared that the universal use of decimal coinage and weights and measures was only a question of time. How right he was. Edward III tried to convince his English subjects of the advantages of decimals. His French subjects were already converted, but the English were not, and Edward's persuasions came to nothing. Sir Isaac Newton, when he was Master of the Mint, did no better.

In the nineteenth century Charles Babbage with his friend John Herschel tried to work out a calculating machine to take decimals, but never got it made. When John Herschel became Master of the Mint it seemed that decimal currency might come, but opposition proved too strong. Some people at the time believed that twelve pence represented the twelve apostles, and to remove two of them (to make a unit of ten) would be blasphemy. However, Sir John Herschel did introduce the florin, which was one-tenth of £1, and

BANKING AND ACCOUNTING TABLE		
(or whole new penny table)		
£ s. d.	£p	
1d.	0p	
2d.	1p	
3d.	1p	
4d.	2p	
5d.	2p	
6d.	3p	
7d.	3p	
8d.	3p	
9d.	4p	
10d.	4p	
11d.	5p	
1s.	5p	Exactly equal
1s. 1d.	5p	
1s. 2d.	6p	
1s. 3d.	6p	
1s. 4d.	7p	
1s. 5d.	7p	
1s. 6d.	7p	
1s. 7d.	8p	
1s. 8d.	8p	
1s. 9d.	9p	
1s. 10d.	9p	
1s. 11d.	10p	
2s.	10p	Exactly equal

Convert the largest EVEN number of shillings in a number first, then use the table for the remainder, and add the two amounts together. Thus:

$$4s. 11d. = 20p + 5p = 25p$$
$$5s. 11d. = 20p + 10p (1s. 11d.) = 30p$$

inscribed as such. He knew that later it could serve for an introduction of the decimal system.

The move towards the new currency really started in 1951 when a Board of Trade report on weights and measures included a favourable view on decimalizing the currency. In 1960 came a joint report from the British Association for the Advancement of Science and from the Association of the British Chambers of Commerce supporting a change.

By then many countries had already 'gone decimal': Aden in 1951, the British West Indies in 1955, and India in 1957; South Africa, Botswana, Lesotho, Swaziland, Pakistan, Australia, and New Zealand were planning to do so. In 1961 Pakistan and South Africa went over to the decimal system, and the change proved not to be so formidable as had been feared.

In 1963 the Halsbury Committee was set up to advise on the most convenient and practical form for a decimal currency in Britain. They investigated twenty-five systems and finally narrowed the choice down to four: the £, the 10s., the 5s., and the 8s. 4d. (100 old pence). By a four-to-two majority the committee decided in favour of the £ rather than the 10s. unit, even though South Africa, Australia, and New Zealand had chosen the 10s. unit divided into 100 cents.

The reasons for deciding on the £ with 100 new pence were, first, that changing to 10s. for the major unit meant doubling the numbers used in our pricing system: a new car would cost not £875 but 1,750 units of 10s.; wages would be not £20 per week but 40 units. Secondly, the £ unit was better for business and machine conversion. Thirdly, by introducing 10s. as the new major unit of account we should have *two* new units (the 10s. and the new penny), which would mean the loss of familiar guidelines. Finally, because a large part of the world's trade and insurance risks were made in sterling, international interests like banking, shipping, and insurance strongly supported the retention of the £.

Whatever the arguments for or against the £ or 10s. units may be, the essential point is that changing to a decimal system has great practical advantages in schools, business, and trade.

[*British Museum.*

The Twelve Caesars.

1. Julius Caesar.
2. Augustus.
3. Tiberius.
4. Caligula.

5. Claudius.
6. Nero.
7. Galba.
8. Otho.

9. Vitellius.
10. Vespasian.
11. Titus.
12. Domitian.

12

ROMAN COINS

THE ROMANS USED BRONZE coins. Exchange proved so difficult in areas like Sicily and the south of Italy, where silver was used, that in 187 B.C. a silver coin called a *denarius* was introduced. Weighing one-seventh of an ounce and having a value equivalent to 10 ounces of copper, it bore the letters C and P for the heavenly twins, Castor and Pollux. They were shown on the reverse side galloping into battle with the word ROMA beneath the horses' hooves.

Castor and Pollux were twin sons of Zeus and Leda in Greek mythology. Skilled and brave fighters, they rescued their sister Helen when she was carried off as a child by Theseus. But when Castor and Pollux took part in the expedition of the Argonauts to find the Golden Fleece they themselves carried off the young maidens, Hilaeira and Phoebe, who were both betrothed. In a resultant fight Castor was killed. His brother, an immortal, asked to be allowed to die also. Zeus granted that they should spend alternate days together in Hades and in Heaven. The two brightest stars in the constellation known as Gemini (the twins) are named after them.

The *denarius* became one of the most important coins ever issued; it was copied all over the world and retained in the form of the penny in Britain even after decimalization.

The Romans grew into a great empire and trading nation. As their empire expanded in the second century B.C. they needed more money. More coins were issued with new designs, usually with the face of a god on one side and a special event on the other. Powerful people often had marks or names stamped on the coins to commemorate dates or people in their family history.

Sulla's grandson used both sides of a coin in 59 B.C. to depict triumphs of his grandfather's career. Pompey's sons arranged after their father's murder in 48 B.C. for his portrait to appear on the coins in three denominations he had newly struck in his lifetime.

Julius Caesar, who succeeded Pompey, managed to get the Senate to agree to stamp his portrait on the coinage while he was still alive, but he didn't live to enjoy it very long, for he was murdered in the same year, 44 B.C. The commonest of his coins have an elephant with a raised trunk trampling on a serpent.

After Caesar's death civil war took place between Antony, on the one hand, and Brutus and Cassius, on the other, for the succession. Shakespeare's play *Julius Caesar* tells how Brutus and Cassius committed suicide and Antony and Octavian eventually succeeded. Antony was defeated at Actium in 31 B.C., and he and Queen Cleopatra took their own lives. Coins of all these reigns can still be found, but some are forged.

By 29 B.C. Octavian had become the Emperor Augustus, and his dominions spread far beyond Rome and the Mediterranean. He struck the gold *aureus*, worth 25 silver *denarii*, bearing his portrait. Thereafter it was customary for Roman coins to show the figure of the ruling emperor. The letters S.C. found on coins up to A.D. 253 mean that they were struck with the authority of the Senate.

In St. Matthew's Gospel, chapter 22, we read the following:

'Show me the tribute money. And they brought unto him a penny. And he sayeth unto them, whose is this image and superscription? They say unto him Caesar's. Then sayeth he unto them, Render therefore unto Caesar the things which are Caesar's and unto God the things that are God's.'

[*British Museum.*

Coins of Roman Britain.

1. Carausius, A.D. 286–293, denarius.
2. Allectus, A.D. 293–296, antoninianus.
3. Constantine the Great, A.D. 306–337, follis.
4. Maximian, A.D. 286–305, follis.
5. Magnus Maximus, A.D. 383–388, solidus.
6. Constantine III, A.D. 407–411, solidus.

|The Mansell Collection.

Imperial Roman Coins and Coins of Barbarian Nations.

The Caesar, or Emperor, of that time was Tiberius (A.D. 14–37), and the phrase 'tribute money' refers to the tribute or tax on Judea when it became a province of the Roman empire in A.D. 6. All males between 14 and 65 and all females between 12 and 65 years had to pay this tax in Roman coin. The word penny is a biblical translation of *denarius*, and therefore the coins are known as 'tribute pennies'.

Though fairly common, they are quite expensive to buy, as collectors do not like to part with them. Some were found in England when the Roman baths at Bath, Somerset, were unearthed in the present century. Silver representations of the tribute penny can be bought in the Roman baths today.

Pontius Pilate, who was Governor of Judea during the reign of Tiberius, had, like all procurators (or governors) in charge of the Palestinian provinces of Judea, Samaria, and Idumae after A.D. 6, the privilege of issuing small copper coins with the emperor's name. These coins are rarer than the tribute penny, and eagerly sought by collectors.

Wars and revolutions are bad for coins as well as people. Inferior metal takes the place of good. So it was in the last days of the Roman empire. By A.D. 260, when the Emperor Valerian was captured, the *antoninanus* (originally a silver coin when it took over from the *denarius*) had become bronze thinly coated with silver. There was no silver currency at all; brass and copper coins were no longer issued, and gold was used only for paying the troops.

In A.D. 296 Diocletian finally set up a reliable coinage in gold and silver; but in the fourth century wars and the threat of invasion caused Constantine the Great to transfer the capital from Rome to Byzantium, which was renamed Constantinople (and is now Istanbul).

The sun was setting on the empire of Rome. But the use of coins continued for another 2,000 years.

King Aethelred the Unready pays Danegeld to the Viking invaders of England. A
painting by Eaton Woodville.

13

OLD BRITISH COINS

BRITAIN'S NEW DECIMALIZED money replaces a system of coin counting that has lasted 1,000 years, so a short history of British coinage is given below. Much must be left out: this is a book all about money, not about all money, which would have to be a most gigantic tome, for the British Museum has twenty-nine volumes on Greek coins alone.

The **farthing** was in Anglo-Saxon times merely a unit of account: a 'feorthling' or fourth part of a silver penny. It first appeared as an actual coin in 1279 and again during the reign of Edward III. Queen Mary (1553–58) issued halfpennies and three-farthings but no farthing pieces, so a shortage of small change developed which lasted for many reigns. Traders therefore began to issue their own token coins for small amounts.

In an effort to stop this, James I (1603–25) gave a licence to Lord Harington to manufacture brass farthings. James, however, arranged that instead of issuing farthings through the Royal Mint, Lord Harington would do the job, and share half the profits. James would pocket the other half. However, traders rejected the farthings of Lord Harington, perhaps because they did not care for brass, perhaps they did not care for Lord Harington. His licence eventually passed elsewhere and was finally abandoned. Farthings ceased in 1644, and traders continued trading with

117

their own tokens. A standard copper coin was therefore issued in 1672. This proved expensive, as copper had to be imported from Sweden. For economy reasons a change was made to tin farthings in 1684, but the issue was not successful and lasted only one year.

Bronze farthings came in 1860. The quarter farthings struck in 1839 and 1851–53 for use in the Crown Colonies were the lowest denomination coins ever to be issued in Britain.

The last issue of the farthing was in 1956, and it was demonetized (i.e., withdrawn from circulation and no longer legal tender) in 1960.

The **halfpenny,** introduced with the farthing as a part of the currency from 1280, is thought to have been first issued by Halfdene, a Viking leader, in Saxon times. Documents dating from the time of King Edward the Confessor mention halfpennies, but these might have been the one-third pennies of King Alfred the Great (871–899).

Charles II altered Edward's silver halfpenny into a copper coin bearing on its back a portrait of Britannia; all subsequent half pennies had this portrait until it was replaced in 1937 by Drake's *Golden Hind.*

The **penny** is one of the oldest and most used coins of all, having begun its life in Britain as a silver piece in the reign of King Offa (757–796) of Mercia. Why a silver piece when its predecessor, the *dinar* circulating in Byzantium, was gold? The answer is that the gold supply in the western world was dwindling. It was enough to pay taxes, but not enough for even the limited trade of the seventh century onwards.

As late as A.D. 708 a man called Grasolfo, who actually produced coins for the city of Lucca, paid for a piece of land costing 28 *solidi,* by 15 coins and a horse. He was not trading in an old horse for a new horse, as a man might trade in an old car for a new one today, so this transaction suggests that even an extremely rich man in one of the richest cities of Europe still, in the eighth century, preferred to settle half his debts with something other than coin.

Money to pay for goods or services, or as a means of exchange was not yet widely understood. Plate and jewels were more highly valued as a store of wealth than was a hoard of coins.

The growing shortage of gold meant that silver had to take its place. This is why, although there are three known gold coins of this reign, one a copy of a Byzantine trade coin, King Offa issued silver pennies. By the eighth century gold coins disappeared as a regular currency. Charlemagne adjusted the exchange basis of the old Roman gold *solidus* and introduced a system of money counting (20 *solidi* = 240 *denarii* or silver pence) which lasted in England until Decimalization Day, the term penny still being retained.

A very early penny struck by King Aethelbert of East Anglia (died 794) bears his portrait with a reverse design of wolf and twins copied from the Roman coins of Constantine the Great. Three specimens only of this coin are known.

By contrast, Aethelred II's pennies (978–1016) are quite common because large quantities had to be minted to pay ransom money or *Danegeld* to the Danish pirates to keep away from England's shores: seventy-five mints were needed to meet the demand. But strict control of coin minting had been introduced by earlier kings, Alfred, Edward, and Aethelstan, and even incompetent Aethelred could not easily damage the system.

When William of Normandy conquered Britain in 1066 he kept the well-ordered currency, but to remedy the varying weights of the Anglo-Saxon silver penny he fixed its weight at $22\frac{1}{2}$ grains (about one-twentieth of an ounce). It remained there for the next 200 years. The penny thus became known as a *sterling*, which means in Old English a fixed or strong thing (like the Latin *solidus*), and it had a good reputation abroad. Even today the word 'sterling' survives as the name for English currency in foreign-exchange markets.

King David of Scotland (1124–53) introduced a silver penny in his country, similar to that minted by King Stephen of England (1135–54). Henry III (1216–72) struck a gold penny in 1257, valued first at 20 silver pennies and later at 24. It was a very handsome coin showing the King seated on the throne holding the orb and sceptre with the legend *Henricus Rex III*.

A long cross on the reverse side which extended to the edge made easier the cutting of the coins into halves or quarters for small change. It also helped to show if the coin had been 'clipped' or filed down, a common occurrence in the Middle Ages.

The angles of the cross were decorated with roses and pellets, but even this embellishment did not make the gold penny popular. Very few were issued, so it is among the rarest of British coins. One of the seven known specimens (three are in the British Museum) realized £1,950 when offered for sale in 1955.

Silver pennies, unlike the decorative gold issues, proved very useful, however. They were in great demand on the Continent and often copied. When used for making wool payments to England the forgeries, which showed the king with an uncrowned head, were called *pollards*, derived from the word 'poll', meaning head, or *crockards* from 'crocket', meaning curl.

Later Continental *esterlings* or pennies were copied more precisely even to the crowned head, especially by King John the Blind of Bohemia. Only the legend (or inscription) on the coins saved them from being outright forgeries.

Furthermore, King John spelt his name EIWANES (the Latin for John is Johannes), probably hoping it would be mistaken for the English king's EDWARDUS. In those days when few people could read, fewer still would notice the difference. It is not a habit, even in literate countries, to read coin inscriptions before making a purchase.

Elizabeth I (1558–1603) first struck copper pennies in 1601. They became common after 1797 when Matthew Boulton manufactured them at his Soho, Birmingham, mint. In the next two years more than 1,000 tons of twopenny pieces, pence, halfpence, and farthings were issued. The penny weighed exactly one ounce. The twopenny piece, twice the weight of the penny, became the biggest coin ever to be minted on a large scale. Without Boulton's steam press such a massive issue of such a large coin would have been impossible. Bronze pennies were introduced in 1860.

Edward III introduced **twopenny pieces.** They were small silver coins known as a half-groat. They remained until 1797, when the large copper pieces weighing two ounces (referred to in the previous paragraph) took their place. Known as 'cartwheels', and struck by Matthew Boulton and James Watt, inventor of the steam engine, these large coins were so perfect that forgery was almost impossible.

No twopenny pieces have since been issued, except for use in the British Colonies (in 1838 and 1848) and as *Maundy Money.* From about the fourth century the sovereign on Maundy Thursday (the Thursday before Easter Sunday) customarily washed the feet of a number of poor people, and gave them alms in the form of clothing, food, and money. This was done as a royal act of humility to commemorate Christ washing the feet of his apostles.

The washing rite was discontinued in 1754, but silver pennies continued to be struck for distribution until 1800 when 4*d.*, 3*d.*, 2*d.*, and 1*d.* pieces were used for the ceremony, which takes place annually in Westminster Abbey. The coins are the only British ones still struck in silver.

The **threepenny piece** was introduced as a silver coin in 1551. It showed a delicately engraved portrait of Edward VI flanked by a rose on one side and the denomination in Roman numerals on the other. Mint marks, such as an acorn, bell, coronet, or eglantine, which normally reveal the place of manufacture, give clues as to the date of Elizabeth's threepences, for at this time all coins were minted at the Tower of London. The silver threepence lost popularity on account of its small size, particularly in the present century (except in the West Indies and Scotland, where people may be thriftier, or have a liking for small things) and was demonetized in 1946. Valuable dates for collectors are 1887 and 1893, years when small issues took place.

The first normal issue of the twelve-sided nickel-brass threepences, which took the place of the silver threepence, was in 1937, and featured the head of George VI. There are a small number in existence with the same date and the head of Edward

|Press Association.

Maundy Money bags. The money which the Queen presents to old people on each Maundy Thursday of Easter Week is kept ready in these little bags.

THE NORMAN CONQUEST

British Museum.

The Norman Conquest.
1 & 4. Edward the Confessor.   2 & 5. Harold II.
3 & 6. William I.

VIII. They are rare, and worth perhaps £1,000. The Edward VIII version also differs from the George VI issue on the reverse side, where a thin raised line divides the date and encircles the thrift plant. A very fine 1949 brass threepence might be worth over £30.

The **groat** was originally any thick silver coin, but between 1279 and 1662 it came to be the name given to the fourpenny piece. The first issue under Edward I was a large and beautiful coin, but partly because the moneyers who minted it received no profit, the coin proved unsuccessful and was withdrawn.

From the tenth century onwards, though English coins were issued in the king's name, certain clergy had mints of their own, which were very profitable. Successive kings gradually reduced the number of these ecclesiastical mints. By the fifteenth century only the archbishops of Canterbury and York and the bishops of Durham had minting rights left. Furthermore, the rights were

123

only for the smaller and less profitable coins, such as the groat and half-groat.

They were marked with the initial or badge of the bishop who issued them. Cardinal Wolsey unwittingly added another misdemeanour to those that led him to be accused of treason in 1530, by issuing a large groat which featured his cardinal's hat and the initials T.W.

But any temptation for another bishop or cardinal to do likewise disappeared with the Reformation when all the ecclesiastical mints were suppressed. Thomas Cranmer proved to be the last Archbishop of Canterbury to have his own initials on the coins of the realm.

In 1836 Joseph Hume suggested that a fourpenny coin would be useful for paying London cab fares, and the piece was then reissued, getting the name 'Joey'. Circulation ceased in 1888.

The **sixpence,** introduced in 1551, worked hard and had an average life of twenty-eight years compared with the forty years of a shilling. It was regularly issued from the seventeenth century onwards. The 1878 sixpence has DRITANNIAR on the obverse, and is very rare. The whole issue is thought to have been released in Cyprus. Another rare sixpence is the 1952 mintage of only 1 million coins compared with the normal 20 million per year of George VI's reign, or over 100 million per year of Elizabeth II.

The **shilling** was in use as a unit of account from Saxon times. Henry VII issued it as a coin in 1503. Then known as a *testoon*, it became the first British coin to bear a monarch's recognizable likeness. It has been a regular denomination right up to 1968.

The **florin** began life in the duchy or *ducatus* of Florence in 1252. It equalled the *augustalle*, a gold coin introduced in 1231 by Emperor Frederick II of Germany, who had inherited the kingdoms of Naples and Sicily from his mother. Genoa and Venice also issued similar gold coins.

The gold piece of Florence bore, like all the other coins of the city, a picture of St. John the Baptist on one side of the coin and a lily on the obverse. It became known as the *fiorino* (flower) *d'oro* (of gold) and eventually 'florin'.

[British Museum.

English Silver Coins.

1. William I, penny.   4. Henry VI, groat.   6. Elizabeth I, sixpence.
2. Henry I, penny.   5. Henry VII, shilling. 7. Charles I, half-crown.
3. Edward I, penny.

At this time there had grown up a need for a regular issue of gold coinage as part of the £ *s. d.* currency. Trade was increasing rapidly. Few good coins of high value existed save for the Venetian *ducat* or *grosso*, which equalled 2 *solidii* or 24

125

denarii, and supplied the requirements of traders for a high-value coin.

But it bore no denomination or mark of value, and the authorities could easily alter the value of the *grosso* without changing its size or weight. They merely debased the *denarii*. A new golden florin could therefore have brought a much-needed stability to the currency. But though the florin was gold, other coins were silver. The value of all of them altered according to the different prices of both gold and silver in the market. This is always the danger when coins have their value related to two metals rather than one.

Fortunately, Florence, Venice, and Genoa had large reserves of gold for the new currency. Venice imported goods from around the eastern Mediterranean, paid for them in gold coin, and then sold the goods to Hungary and countries north of the Alps. Later, Venice used the Hungarian payments (which were made in gold bullion) to make her own new gold coin, called the *ducat d'oro* to distinguish it from the silver ducat, or grosso.

The gold ducat and the gold florin became the most important coins in European trade until the fifteenth century, and helped to give the Italian cities an early lead in the history of banking.

In England in the reign of Edward III (1327–77) a gold florin was minted with the value of six shillings. It did not circulate for long, even though it was a beautiful coin showing the seated figure of the King, holding his orb and sceptre, and enthroned beneath a canopy. Fleur-de-lis and leopards' heads were used for decoration.

But just at the time when Edward minted his golden florins King Louis of Hungary began issuing masses of the gold he had been storing for years, so that even today King Louis' coins are the commonest of medieval gold coins. This meant that in 1344 nobody wanted English florins: they were overvalued. Many of them were melted down. Today they are among the rarest and most beautiful of English coins. They were superseded by the *noble*, one of the few coins to depict a naval victory, that of the Battle of Sluys in 1340.

Many of the *nobles* were minted at Calais, which was an important centre for wool exports.

A two-shilling piece was struck in 1848 as the thin edge of the wedge for the introduction of decimal currency. Although decimal coinage did not materialize for another 120 years, the florin remained. The words DEI GRATIA were left out of the inscription on the first 750,000, which therefore became known as the 'Godless florins'.

In 1851 the words went on, and a broader and thinner coin came into use. Britannia appeared as a standing instead of a seated figure between 1902 and 1910, for the first and only time. Almost all pre-1933 florins are worth more, sometimes very much more, than their face value.

The **half-crown** was issued by Henry VII as a gold coin, and by Edward VI as a silver one, along with crowns, sixpences, and threepences. In the Civil War (1642–45) some were struck to supply towns under the control of the Royalists. The best known of these 'siege pieces' is the lozenge-shaped half-crown. Some odd denominations, such as 2s. 2d., 1s. 3d., 11d., and 7d., turned up because the value of the coin depended on the weight of the metal, which was variable. Silver-pound sovereigns worth 20s. were struck at this time; with a diameter of 2 inches and weighing $3\frac{3}{4}$ ounces, they are the largest silver coins ever to be issued.

During the period 1851–73 only a few proof half-crowns, some of which went overseas, were struck. Because they are so uncommon they are quite valuable. Rarest of the half-crown family was the 1952 issue, only one of which is known to exist. It is now in the United States, with a market value of £2,200. Other dates worth looking for (and with more hope of success than a 1952 find) are 1905, of which 0·2 million were minted, and 1925, of which 1·4 million were minted. The half-crown was demonetized in 1969.

A **double florin** was issued in 1887 as part of Queen Victoria's jubilee coinage. Being bulky and too similar to the crown, it was discontinued in 1890.

The **crown** was struck as a gold coin by Henry VIII, perhaps to atone for having reduced the weight of the gold sovereign. It was copied from the French *écu*, a popular coin in Europe. Early

English Gold Coins.

1. Henry III, gold penny.
2. Edward III, noble.
3. Henry VI, angel.
4. Henry VII, sovereign.
5. Charles II, guinea.

crowns have the initials H.K. for Henry and his first wife, Katharine of Aragon. Later issues bear H.A. for Anne Boleyn, and H.I. for Jane Seymour.

Though the crown had a large circulation, it was replaced by a

128

silver coin in Edward VI's reign, because gold supplied by Wales and Cornwall to the Royal Mint was running low. This silver crown bears the date 1551, but shillings issued by Edward have been found with an earlier date still: 1545. Crowns with an English instead of a Latin legend were issued by Parliament after 1649, and a regular issue minted from 1662. In 1818 a new crown featuring St. George and the dragon was struck, perhaps derived from the Henry VIII coin called a 'George noble', which showed St. George slaying the dragon. The 'half-George noble' had a similar design.

From 1937 onwards, crowns were used for commemorative issues only: in 1951 (the 400th anniversary of the silver crown's introduction into the British coinage), one was issued for the Festival of Britain. In 1953 came another for Queen Elizabeth II's coronation. This one, like the first crown of Edward VI, shows the monarch as an equestrian figure. The 1965 crown carries the portrait of Sir Winston Churchill on the reverse instead of Britannia or St. George.

In 1560 Eloye Mestrelle, a discharged employee of the Paris Mint, began work in London. For eleven years he struck gold and silver coins, not by hand, but by presses powered by horses. The coins were much better than the previous hand-hammered ones, but handworkers feared that if machine coins were introduced they would lose their jobs. So Mestrelle lost his instead.

Hand-made coins came back in 1572, and, sadly, Mestrelle was hanged in 1578 for counterfeiting. His fate reminds us that counterfeiting has always been regarded as a serious crime. But during the Second World War convicted counterfeiters in Germany were used to produce forged Allied bank-notes. The operation, under the code name 'Bernhard', involved £150 million worth of Bank of England notes. The forgers did their work so well that the English temporarily stopped issuing white £5 notes.

Machine minting, feared in the sixteenth century, became acceptable in the seventeenth, and in 1660 the production of coins by hand ceased. The change to mechanical minting was the most important one in the history of English coinage until decimalization.

The new milled coins weighed slightly less than the old hammered ones, but they could not be easily clipped. Mass production was now possible, provided enough silver could be found. Louis XIV of France provided this by buying Dunkirk under the Treaty of Dover, 1662. He paid for his purchase with $1\frac{1}{2}$ million *écus d'argent*, all of which were turned over to the Mint.

Perhaps because the origin of the silver was slightly unsavoury, the coins made from it were not marked in any way, whereas later coins, if of unusual origin, often revealed their source. Thus silver sixpences of Queen Anne's reign made from bullion captured at Vigo Bay (1702) bore the word VIGO to indicate where the silver had come from.

The South Sea Company's initials were placed on silver coins of George I, and the East India Company's initials on gold coins of George II, when those companies brought the metal to the Mint.

Guineas worth 20 shillings, minted by Pierre Blondeau, were among the first denominations to come off the new press. The source of the gold for the guineas was Guinea in Africa. They therefore had an elephant or elephant and castle below the bust of the king, for the elephant and castle were the emblem of the African Trading Company which delivered the gold to the Mint. The guinea kept its name after the gold came from other sources, but its value veered from 20 to 30 shillings owing to changes in the relative prices of silver and gold. In 1717 it became stabilized at 21 shillings, at which price it remained until 1816 when displaced by the sovereign.

The last guinea was struck in 1813 to supply Wellington's army in the Peninsular War, but even when the coin finally disappeared from circulation, the term guinea remained as a unit of account for 21 shillings.

In 1489, during the reign of Henry VII, a new gold coin called a **sovereign,** worth 20 shillings, was struck. Copied from the *real d'or* of the Netherlands, it was the first coin to have the value of a pound sterling. It was large (diameter $1\frac{2}{3}$ inches) and heavy (weighing $\frac{1}{2}$ ounce), so that the King could be portrayed in all his glory. His son, Henry VIII, spent a great deal, and soon the gold and silver content of all the coins was reduced. Edward VI, Mary, and Elizabeth I successively tried to remedy the situation. Values were finally marked down so that the coins again became standard: their face value equalling their weight. Gold coins appeared only sporadically during the next two centuries. By 1816 a most complicated coinage had arisen. Because silver was in short supply, the Mint had bought some Spanish coins and overstamped them with George III's head, hardly a handsome sight at the best of times, and certainly not more beautiful on a Spanish dollar. A whole new system of coinage was therefore introduced.

The Royal Mint, with steam-powered machinery, went from cramped quarters in the Tower to a new site at Tower Hill. The gold coinage was altered. The 21s. guinea disappeared. New coins, sovereigns and half-sovereigns, beautifully designed by the Italian medallist, Benedetto Pistrucci, came in. But a more important changeover than design took place.

For years Britain had had a dual standard of silver and gold. Now the currency was to be measured in one metal only, gold. The gold content of the sovereign was worth one pound sterling. All the other coins were related to the value of gold.

George IV preferred a formal coat of arms on his coins, so Pistrucci's St. George disappeared from the sovereign in 1825. He came back complete with dragon, however, in 1871, when discoveries of gold in Australia and South Africa meant that gold was plentiful and more coins could be struck. Many were minted in these two countries, including in 1894, in South Africa, 216 threepenny pieces, the lowest denomination gold coin ever issued. They are now worth over 16,000 times their face value.

The gold sovereign circulated along with bank-notes and was interchangeable with them until war broke out in 1914. Sovereigns were then replaced entirely by Treasury notes, i.e. notes issued not by the Bank of England as was normal but by the Treasury. In 1925 paper notes were again exchangeable for gold, but only in amounts of more than 400 ounces. Even this exchange was abolished in 1931, and gold retained only for the payment of international debts.

In George VI's time the only gold coins were proof sets of £5 and £2 pieces, and sovereigns and half sovereigns, struck in 1937. In Elizabeth II's reign £10 million gold sovereigns were issued to form part of Britain's gold reserves (or savings). Gold coins no longer circulate, and even to hold four gold coins minted after 1837 it is necessary to have a collector's licence.

The term **sterling** derived from the penny of William the Conqueror, which had a fixed weight for two centuries. The weight of 20 silver pennies eventually became accepted as a standard of both weight and value. Though changes in coinage names, and weights have taken place, the pound sterling remains an international money standard against which other countries' currencies are valued.

14

CURRENCIES AND EXCHANGE RATES THROUGHOUT THE WORLD

SO FAR WE HAVE MENTIONED only two present-day currencies—the pound and the dollar. But of course there are many different monetary systems in use throughout the world. Some are very important in international trade, while others are seldom heard of outside their country of origin. The currencies of some 120 countries are listed in the accompanying table.

It will be seen at once that nearly every one of the countries listed has a *decimal* currency: in other words, the main coin or note is divided into 100 (or, occasionally, 1,000) parts.

The table also shows that different countries often use the same name for their currencies. Thus there are several different dollars, pounds, francs, rupees, krone, etc. We have to be careful, therefore, when we are speaking of 'dollars' to indicate whether we mean, for example, a United States dollar or an Australian dollar. We have to be careful to distinguish between, say, a Swiss franc and a Belgian franc; between a Mexican peso and a Cuban peso.

Anyone who is interested in the history of money can spend an absorbing and useful half-hour discovering, with the aid of a good dictionary, the origins of the currencies named in the table. For example, the word 'dollar' is derived by way of the *taler* (an old European coin) from the name *Joachimstal*, a town which supplied silver to the Austrian mint. The dollar symbol $ probably

[*Radio Times Hulton Picture Library.*

William Penn's treaty with the Indians. A painting by B. West.

came from the figure 8 on the gold 8-*real* pieces or Spanish dollars (the traditional 'pieces of eight'). The pound sign £ is a form of the letter L from the Latin word *libra* meaning 'pound' as a weight. The Italian lira is also derived from the *libra*; hence we sometimes find the £ symbol used in Italy for lira.

The table includes a rough indication of how much the various currencies are worth in sterling. We have to bear in mind that this is no more than a guide, because rates of exchange are constantly fluctuating. Some countries may find it necessary to *devalue* their money tomorrow (in which case it can be bought more cheaply abroad), while it is just possible that some other currencies may be *revalued* and thus become more expensive abroad.

Most European countries developed their currencies from the heritage of the Greeks and the Romans. As in Britain, ecclesiastical (church) and royal mints were established for the production of coins, and central banks for the issue of notes. But countries without their own mints began trading first by barter, then using either tokens or acceptable coins of foreign countries, until finally they were able to establish their own currencies.

134

CURRENCIES AROUND THE WORLD

Country	Currency	
	Main unit	Comprising
Albania	lek	100 qintar
Algeria	dinar	100 centimes
Andorra	peseta	100 centimos
Angola	escudo	100 centavos
Antigua	dollar	100 cents
Argentina	peso	100 centavos
Australia	dollar	100 cents
Austria	schilling	100 groschen
Azores	escudo	100 cents
Bahamas	dollar	100 cents
Bahrain	dinar	1,000 fils
Barbados	dollar	100 cents
Belgium	franc	100 centimes
Bermuda	pound	$20s. = 240d.$
Bolivia	peso	100 centavos
Botswana	rand	100 cents
Brazil	cruzeiro	100 centavos
British Honduras	dollar	100 cents
Brunei	dollar	100 cents
Bulgaria	lev	100 stotinki
Burma	kyat	100 pyas
Cambodia	riel	100 sen
Canada	dollar	100 cents
Ceylon	rupee	100 cents
Chile	escudo	100 centesimos
Colombia	peso	100 centavos
Costa Rica	colon	100 centimos
Cuba	peso	100 centavos
Cyprus	pound	1,000 mils
Czechoslovakia	crown	100 heller
Denmark	krone	100 ore
Ecuador	sucre	100 centavos
Egypt	pound	100 piastres
Ethiopia	dollar	100 cents
Fiji	dollar	100 cents
Finland	markka	100 pennis
France	franc	100 centimes
Gambia	pound	$20s. = 240d.$
Germany (West)	Deutschemark	100 pfennig

CURRENCIES AROUND THE WORLD—*continued*

Country	Currency	
	Main unit	*Comprising*
Ghana	new cedi	100 pesewas
Gibraltar	pound	20s. = 240d.
Greece	drachma	100 lepta
Guatemala	quetzal	100 centavos
Guyana	dollar	100 cents
Haiti	gourde	100 centimes
Hong Kong	dollar	100 cents
Hungary	forint	100 filler
Iceland	krona	100 aurar
India	rupee	100 paise
Iran	rial	100 dinars
Iraq	dinar	1,000 fils
Ireland (Eire)	pound	20s. = 240d.
Israel	pound	100 agorot
Italy	lira	100 centesimi
Jamaica	dollar	100 cents
Japan	yen	100 sen
Jordan	dinar	1,000 fils
Kenya	shilling	100 cents
Kuwait	dinar	1,000 fils
Lebanon	pound	100 piastres
Lesotho	rand	100 cents
Liberia	U.S. dollar	100 cents
Libya	pound	1,000 mill.
Luxemburg	franc	100 centimes
Malawi	pound	20s. = 240d.
Malaysia	dollar	100 cents
Malta	pound	20s. = 240d.
Mauritius	rupee	100 cents
Mexico	peso	100 centavos
Monaco	franc	100 centimes
Morocco	dirham	100 francs
Nepal	rupee	100 pice
Netherlands	guilder	100 cents
New Guinea	dollar	100 cents
Nicaragua	cordoba	100 centavos
Nigeria	pound	20s. = 240d.
Norway	krone	100 ore
Pakistan	rupee	100 paisa
Panama	balboa	100 centesimos

Currencies and Exchange Rates Throughout the World

Country	Currency	
	Main unit	*Comprising*
Papua	dollar	100 cents
Paraguay	guarani	100 centimos
Peru	sol	100 centavos
Philippines	peso	100 centavos
Poland	zloty	100 grosze
Portugal	escudo	100 centavos
Puerto Rico	U.S. dollar	100 cents
Rhodesia	pound	$20s. = 240d.$
Romania	leu	100 bani
St. Kitts	dollar	100 cents
St. Lucia	dollar	100 cents
St. Vincent	dollar	100 cents
Samoa	dollar	100 cents
Saudi Arabia	riyal	20 gurshes = 100 halalah
Seychelles	rupee	100 cents
Sierra Leone	leone	100 cents
Singapore	dollar	100 cents
Solomon Islands	dollar	100 cents
Somalia	shilling	100 cents
South Africa	rand	100 cents
South West Africa	rand	100 cents
Spain	peseta	100 centimos
Sudan	pound	100 piastres
Swaziland	rand	100 cents
Sweden	krona	100 ore
Switzerland	franc	100 centimes
Syria	pound	100 piastres
Tahiti	franc	100 centimes
Tanzania	shilling	100 cents
Thailand	baht	100 satang
Tonga	dollar	100 cents
Trinidad and Tobago	dollar	100 cents
Tunisia	dinar	1,000 mill
Turkey	pound	100 piastres
Uganda	shilling	100 cents
United States	dollar	100 cents
U.S.S.R.	rouble	100 kopecks
Uruguay	peso	100 centesimos
Venezuela	bolivar	100 centimos
Yugoslavia	dinar	100 paras
Zambia	kwacha	100 ngwee

Early settlers in **Australia,** for example, used English, Dutch, Portuguese, Asiatic, and Spanish coins. When, in 1813, a quantity of Spanish 8-*real* pieces arrived, Governor Macquarie ordered their centres to be punched. The resultant rings and discs (or plugs) circulated together; the former, known as the 'holey dollars', being worth 5*s.*, the latter 1*s.* 3*d.* They were easily counterfeited, and though an effort to withdraw them was made in 1822, they circulated until 1829, when they were worth 3*s.* 3*d.* and 1*s.* 1*d.*, respectively.

A quantity of British coins sent to Sydney from the Royal Mint in London proved insufficient for trade; by 1857 the principal currency in Australia was private tokens, usually half-ounce copper pennies and quarter-ounce halfpennies. These and all other private tokens became illegal after 1860 when large amounts of pennies and halfpennies were imported from England.

In 1855 a branch of the Royal Mint was opened in Sydney; and later, Melbourne (1872) and Perth (1899) also had mints. The Sydney mint struck sovereigns and half-sovereigns from the gold discovered in New South Wales and Victoria in 1851. The dies, cut in London, were designed by James Wyon. They showed the young head of Queen Victoria, while instead of the usual St. George and the dragon, the reverse bore the word AUSTRALIA, a crown with SYDNEY MINT ONE SOVEREIGN (or half-sovereign) and an encircling wreath.

Small change was still insufficient for the needs of an expanding territory. One million each of florins, shillings, and sixpences, and 2 million threepences were therefore supplied from the London Mint in 1910. They bore Edward VII's portrait on the obverse, and the Australian arms with kangaroo and emu on the reverse. Pennies, halfpennies, and more silver were sent out in 1911.

In 1916 Australia produced her own silver coins, and in 1919 the Melbourne Mint also issued copper coins, which until that date had been struck in Calcutta. Denominations struck in Bombay, Denver, and San Francisco during the Second World War have their own mint marks.

Crowns were issued in 1937 and 1938, while commemorative

florins were struck in 1927 for the opening of the new Parliament at Canberra, in 1935 for the centenary of Melbourne and Victoria, and in 1954 for the visit of Queen Elizabeth. Australia went over to a decimal system in 1966, using a dollar (worth 10s. of the old currency) divided into 100 cents.

New Zealand, like Australia, began trading by barter, using tobacco, pigs, blankets, and agricultural tools. International trading coins, mainly English, Spanish, American, French, and Indian, were also acceptable.

The Treaty of Waitangi between the Maoris and the British in 1840 established sterling as the national coinage, but no coins were produced especially for New Zealand until 1933. Tokens were therefore widely used. By 1897, when they were finally demonetized, 140 different kinds of token were in circulation. Australian and British money, particularly the groat, had to supply the need for small change. The 1933 issue was minted in London and showed the New Zealand coat of arms on the half-crown, the kiwi bird on the florin, a Maori warrior on the shilling, a huia bird on the sixpence, and carved patu clubs on the three-pence. Pennies and halfpennies were struck in 1940.

A limited number of crown pieces was issued in 1935 to commemorate the Jubilee of King George V. Other crown issues appeared in 1949 (for the visit of King George VI, which did not in fact take place) and 1953 to commemorate the coronation of Queen Elizabeth II. A half-crown was struck in 1940 to mark the centenary of the Treaty of Waitangi.

When decimalization took place in 1967 the two-cent coins, owing to an error, bore the words 'Bahama Islands', and were recalled. The few that got into circulation are worth over £70 each. New Zealand, like Australia, chose the dollar (worth 10s.) as the basis of its decimal currency. The smallest coin, the bronze one cent, features the fern leaf. The two-cent bronze coin shows the kowhai flower, which blooms on one of the country's few deciduous trees. On the five-cent piece is the tuatari, a descendant and last survivor of prehistoric giant reptiles.

The 10-cent coin shows a Maori carved head. The kiwi appears on the 20-cent piece, with a fern in the background; and Captain Cook's ship *Endeavour* is shown on the 50-cent piece. A commemorative dollar with fern leaves enclosing the New Zealand coat of arms, and with the words 'Decimal Currency introduced July 10th, 1967' stamped on the edge, makes up the seventh coin in the New Zealand decimal set.

Both Australia and New Zealand, perhaps drawing on the experience of South Africa, completed their decimal changeover in a shorter period than planned, Australia in eighteen months instead of two years, and New Zealand in ten months instead of eighteen.

Early settlers in **North America** traded by barter. Strings of shells, or 'wampum', often passed for payment, as did furs, goats, and fish. Even as late as 1840, the marriage fee in Iowa was three goatskins or four bushels of sweet potatoes. English, French, Dutch, and Spanish coins were acceptable, especially along the eastern seaboard. Spanish 8-*real* pieces (called dollars) struck at the mints of Mexico and Lima were among the most popular of all. The reverse of the coin had two pillars with intertwined mottoes, and one theory is that the dollar sign originated from this motif (the usual theory is that S is a modification of the 8 from '8-*real*').

The earliest coins to be struck for the British colonies in North America were those for Somers Islands, now Bermuda, in the seventeenth century. Made of silvered brass, they were known as 'hog money' because Sir George Somers, shipwrecked on the Islands in 1609, discovered them to be overrun with pigs.

The first mainland coins were silver shillings, sixpences, and threepences struck in 1652 on behalf of the General Council of Massachusetts. Because of their simple design, the letters NE in script capitals inside a small rectangle on one side, and the value in Roman numerals similarly enclosed on the other, they were easily counterfeited. A more complicated design took their place in 1787 and 1788, but a year later the unprofitable mint closed.

Lord Baltimore issued in 1658 a small quantity of silver shillings, sixpences, and groats; with a few pennies in copper, of which only three examples are known. Mark Newby, an immigrant from Dublin, arrived in New Jersey in 1681, bringing with him a large quantity of Irish copper coins. These were later made legal tender for amounts up to 5s., and became known as 'St. Patrick's halfpence' because they bore a figure of the saint on the obverse.

Token coins circulated in America, as in Australia, New Zealand, and Britain, when there was insufficient small change for trade. So William Wood obtained a patent from George I in 1722 to strike 300 tons of copper twopences, pennies, and halfpennies: 200 tons in the first four years and not more than 10 tons a year for the next ten years. The first coins were undated, but later issues have the dates 1722 and 1723 on them. William Wood also produced copper halfpennies for Ireland in 1724, but the Irish refused to accept them, and these, too, were sent to America.

A much-sought-after American issue is the design by William Moulton for a copper coinage, requested by the House of Representatives in 1776. Because it was never approved, only a few coins, all very rare, passed into circulation.

Under the Articles of Confederation, 1778, each of the American states retained the right to strike its own coins, while Congress regulated their alloys and values. In 1785 Congress passed a resolution that the nation's currency was to be based on the decimal system, the units being dollars and cents. In 1786 came approval for the first issue of copper coins, the 'fugio' cents of 1787, so-called because they showed a sun-dial and the word *fugio*, taken to mean 'time flies'.

In 1791 Congress authorized the establishment of a mint at Philadelphia, and in the following year the first coins (dismes and half-dismes) were struck from silver allegedly supplied by George Washington himself. In 1795 came the gold 10-dollar eagle; the half- and quarter-eagle appeared in 1796. Nearly two million double eagles, each weighing more than four sovereigns, appeared in 1850, possibly as a result of the Californian gold discoveries in 1848. Except for the years 1917–19, they were struck annually until 1933, when America went off the gold standard.

Canada used farm produce and 'wampum' for early barter transactions. American dollars became acceptable, including, on Prince Edward Island, a 'holey dollar' similar to those issued in Australia under Governor Macquarie. The centres circulated at 1s., until the metal was discovered to be worth 1s. 3d. Most of them were rushed back to England for melting, but the ship carrying them was wrecked; the few remaining centres are extremely valuable.

Token coins were struck in England during the nineteenth century to help the expanding trade of Canadian towns such as Quebec, Halifax, and Montreal. Local banks and companies followed suit, and in 1820 the North West Company issued a token worth one beaver pelt. Hudson's Bay Company in 1857 also gave out tokens for 1, $\frac{1}{2}$, $\frac{1}{4}$, and $\frac{1}{8}$ of 'a made beaver skin', which itself was the unit of currency in the Company's forts. The Bank of Montreal issued a number of pennies and halfpennies in 1838 depicting the side and front of the bank. The manager disliked the design and withdrew the coins, so only a few exist today.

Decimal currency was adopted by the Province of Canada in 1858, and by Nova Scotia and New Brunswick in 1860. In 1861 cents and half-cents were struck at the Royal Mint in London and shipped out to New Brunswick. But it was discovered that the half-cents had never been ordered, so they were returned to London. A few still exist because they became mixed with similar coins struck for Nova Scotia, and were returned to Canada.

Prince Edward Island adopted decimal currency in 1871 and issued one denomination: the cent, the only Canadian coin to have the Queen's title in English. Unusually, too, it does not have the mark H, although it was struck at Heaton's mint in Birmingham.

The Dominion of Canada was formed in 1867, Prince Edward Island joining in 1873. Five-, 10-, 25-, and 50-cent pieces, dated 1870, were issued, the design changing in later years. In 1901 a Canadian mint was set up in Ottawa, and British sovereigns struck there have the letter c above the date.

The five-cent piece was struck as a twelve-sided instead of a round coin in 1942, and in 1951 a special five-cent coin was issued to commemorate the 200th anniversary of the isolation of nickel by a Swedish chemist. (Canada has some of the largest nickel deposits in the world.)

The Canadian dollar was first struck in 1935 to mark the twenty-fifth anniversary of George V's accession. Other commemorative dollars were issued in 1939 for the visit of King George VI; in 1949 for the anniversary of Newfoundland's entry into the Confederation; and in 1958 for the centenary of British Columbia as a crown colony.

In the **West Indies** during the seventeenth century, the Spanish dollar or 8-*real* piece was valued at roughly 5*s*. (like an English crown). It was divided into varying fractions according to whether Britain, France, Holland, or Spain controlled the islands. One *real*, worth a few pence, was known as a 'bit'.

An acute currency shortage in the eighteenth and nineteenth centuries meant that coins of other countries were often overstamped or cut to make them legal tender. Eight-*real* pieces and French and Portuguese coins brought to the islands by traders, and pirates (who sometimes made their base in the Caribbean) were commonly used.

Martinique, a French possession until the English occupation of 1797, had a dollar punched with a heart-shaped hole; the plug and the ring circulated along with coins for smaller denominations. The island of St. Lucia had coins both cut and counterstamped, those used in Tortola in the Leeward Islands being known as 'saints'.

Because of its early associations with Greece and Rome, and its situation on early trade routes, **North Africa** has a long and complex history of coinage. **Central** and **South Africa** were more remote from shipping routes until the sixteenth and seventeenth centuries, when the Portuguese, the Dutch, and the British competed for trade.

The African Company of Merchants, formed in England in 1750, issued some silver coins in 1796 for use on the Gold Coast, but they appear not to have circulated widely. Sierra Leone had more early coins, for in 1791 the Sierra Leone Company issued silver dollars, 50, 20, 10, and 5 cents, and copper cents and pennies. In 1907 a coinage of cupro-nickel pennies and tenths of pennies was struck for Nigeria, and in 1913 a general coinage was issued for the whole of what was then British West Africa (Gold Coast, Sierra Leone, Nigeria, and dependencies west of Lake Chad). Silver florins, shillings, sixpences, and threepences, and cupro-nickel pennies, halfpennies, and $\frac{1}{10}$ pennies were issued almost every year thereafter until the emergence of Ghana, Nigeria, and other parts of Africa as independent states in 1957 and 1960. Designs show groundnuts, palm trees, cocoa pods, and cotton flowers.

In **East Africa,** Kenya, Uganda, and Tanganyika had an early coinage authorized by the British East Africa Company. It consisted of the silver rupee and its fractions, together with copper *pice* or quarter *annas*. In 1897 the British Indian rupee became the basis of the currency, having the young head of Queen Victoria and the words EAST AFRICAN PROTECTORATE. After the First World War British coinage was introduced. This was based on the florin divided into 100 cents. In 1921 the shilling became the standard, so that the 50-cent coin reads HALF SHILLING. Some five- and ten-cent coins were struck during the short reign of Edward VIII. On independence, Tanganyika took the name Tanzania.

Prince Henry the Navigator of Portugal opened up the west and south coasts of Africa to European traders. The English captured the Cape in 1795, returned it to the Dutch under the Treaty of Amiens in 1802, and bought it back again with Guiana for £6 million in 1806.

Many different coins circulated in **South Africa,** including those of the Dutch East India Company, of Portugal, Spain, and America. In 1874 President Burgers arranged with a private firm in England to have 265 ounces of gold made into 865 coins, the first gold money ever struck for South Africa.

The gold 'ponds', 'half-ponds', and silver crowns dated 1892 were struck in Berlin to hasten the issue. It was these which contained the error mentioned on page 95.

144

By 1900 the Pretoria Mint had issued 2,600,000 one-pound and half-pound pieces, valued at more than £2,400,000. The pound (or sovereign) ceased in 1932, the half-sovereign ceased in 1926; but other denominations continued, and a crown was added in 1947.

South Africa was the first of several countries to change from an £ *s. d.* coinage to a decimal system. She chose the rand (worth 10*s.*), divided into 100 cents. Changeover was completed by 1966. It was thought originally that 30 million decimal bronze coins would be sufficient for small change. But the 1-rand silver coin was hoarded because of its novelty, and firms were able to change over to decimals more quickly than had been thought possible, so a shortage of small change developed. By the end of 1961 the number of bronze coins reached 100 million: more than three times what had been thought to be an adequate number.

In 1965 a new range of decimal money was phased in: three bank-notes (for one, five, and ten rand), and seven coins. The obverse side of the coins have on them the head of Jan van Riebeck, the first commander of the Cape when it was established in 1652 as a victualling station for ships of the Dutch East India Company. The obverse of the 1-rand coin shows South Africa's national animal, the springbok; the 5-cent coin shows the blue crane; the 10-cent, the aloe; the 20-cent, two varieties of the protea plant; while the 50-cent coin shows an arum lily, *Agapanthus strelizia.* The 2-cent bronze coin shows a wildebeest, and the bronze cent shows two sparrows from the Biblical reference of St. Matthew: 'Are not two sparrows sold for a farthing?' Half of the notes and coins bear the words 'South Africa', while the others bear the word 'Suid Afrika'. This is because South Africa has two official languages: English and Afrikaans.

India broke up in the second century A.D. into many kingdoms, each becoming important in turn. Timur (Tamerlane the Great) occupied India in 1399. So did a descendant of his, Babar, in 1526. Babar and successive emperors issued coins in gold, silver, and copper. A square silver rupee was struck at the Lahore mint under Akbar I (1556–1605), most rupees of this time being circular. Akbar's son, Jahangar, produced twelve gold coins known as zodiacal mohurs because they portrayed the signs of the zodiac. Zodiacal silver rupees were also issued, and both are among the rarest of Indian coins.

Meanwhile, trade with European markets had begun as a result of Vasco da Gama's discovery of the sea route to India in 1497. The East India Company, which was set up to trade with the East, issued coinage in 1600. The four coins ($\frac{1}{8}$, $\frac{1}{4}$, half-dollar, and dollar) had a portcullis design on the obverse, so they are known as portcullis money. They had a limited circulation. The Madras Mint, established in the seventeenth century, reckoned not in dollars but in *pagodas* and fractions of a *pagoda*, such as the *fanam, faluce,* and *cash.* This system ended in 1818, when the rupee became the official unit of currency.

In 1835 gold coins known as the mohur and the double mohur, showing the head of William IV, were struck for the East India Company. Along with silver rupees, half-rupees, quarter-rupees, and two-anna pieces, and copper coins of lower worth, they became generally acceptable.

In 1858 the Company was abolished and all its rights were taken over by the Queen of England. Thereafter the words 'East India Company' on coins were replaced by 'Victoria Queen', and from 1876 by 'Victoria Empress'. However, some states, such as Hyderabad, kept the right to issue their own coins, which often bore the head of their ruler.

In 1946 nickel rupees were issued. Pakistan and India became separate states in 1947. India adopted a decimal currency, based on the rupee divided into 100 paise, in 1957; Pakistan changed over to a similar system in 1961.

SOME SUGGESTED BOOKS

Becker, Thomas W., THE COIN MAKERS. Oak Tree Press: London, and Doubleday, New York, 1969.

Berry, George, DISCOVERING COINS. Shire Publications: Hertfordshire, 1968.

Brown, Laurence, COIN COLLECTING. Mayflower Books: London, 1969.

Carson, R. A. G., COINS: ANCIENT, MEDIAEVAL AND MODERN. Hutchinson: London, 1962.

Gillet Bros. Discount Co., THE BILL ON LONDON. Chapman & Hall: London, 1964.

Hanson, J. L., A TEXTBOOK OF ECONOMICS. (2nd edn.) Macdonald & Evans: London, 1956.

Linecar, Howard, BEGINNER'S GUIDE TO COIN COLLECTING. Sphere Books: London, 1968.

Marshall, B. V., COMPREHENSIVE ECONOMICS. Longmans Green: London, 1967.

Narbeth, Colin, COLLECTING PAPER MONEY. Lutterworth Press: London, 1968.

Porteous, John, COINS IN HISTORY: A SURVEY OF COINAGE FROM THE REFORM OF DIOCLETIAN TO THE LATIN MONETARY UNION. Weidenfeld & Nicolson: London, 1969.

Purvey, Frank, COLLECTING COINS. Foyle: London, 1968.

Sutherland, C. H. V., GOLD: ITS BEAUTY, POWER AND ALLURE. Thames & Hudson: London, 1969.

Wood, D. Neville, DECIMAL CURRENCY FOR BRITAIN. Ward Lock: London, 1967.

Whitehead, Geoffrey, COMMERCE MADE SIMPLE. W. H. Allen: London, 1969.

MUSEUMS WHERE
COIN COLLECTIONS
MAY BE SEEN

ENGLAND

Bedfordshire

Elstow, Moot Hall.

Berkshire

Borough Museum, Old County Hall, Abingdon.
Borough Museum, Newbury.
Borough Museum, Reading.

Buckinghamshire

County Museum, Aylesbury.
High Wycombe Museum, High Wycombe.

Cambridgeshire

Fitzwilliam Museum, Cambridge. (Large collection; all periods.)

Cheshire

Grosvenor Museum, Chester. (Roman; Chester Mint.)
Macclesfield Museum, Hare Hill, Macclesfield.

Cornwall

Borough Museum, Helston.

Penlee Museum, Morrab Road, Penzance.

Derbyshire

Buxton Museum, Buxton.

Chesterfield Public Library and Museum, Corporation Street, Chesterfield.

Heathcote Museum, Brichover, Matlock.

Derby Museum, Wardwick. (Tutbury Hoard; Saxon coins of Derby Mint.)

Devon

Woolcombe House Museum, Sidmouth.

South Molton Museum, South Molton.

Dorset

Pitt Rivers Museum, Farnham, Blandford. (Roman.)

Borough Museum, South Street, Bridport.

County Museum, Dorchester. (Roman.)

Philpot Museum, Lyme Regis.

Poole Museum, South Road, Poole.

Local History Museum, Gold Hill, Shaftesbury.

Durham

Darlington Museum, Tubwell Road, Darlington. (Pennies of Durham Mint.)

Cathedral Library, Durham Great Lumley Treasure Trove. (Elizabeth I.)

Saltwell Park Museum, Saltwell Towers, Gateshead 8.

Sunderland Museum, Borough Road, Sunderland.

Chester Hall, Stockton-on-Tees.

Public Library and Museum, Ocean Road, South Shields.

Gray Art Museum, Clarence Road, West Hartlepool.

Essex

Epping Forest Museum, Queen Elizabeth's Hunting Lodge, Rangers Road, Chingford.

Prittlewell Priory, Southend-on-Sea.

Thurrock Local History Museum, Civic Square, Tilbury.

Gloucestershire

City Museum, Queen's Road, Bristol 8. (Roman; Bristol Mint.)

Cheltenham College Museum, Bath Road, Cheltenham.

City Museum, Gloucester. (Anglo Saxon, Roman and medieval.)

Filkins and Broughton Museum, Filkins, Lechlade.

Hampshire

Willis Museum, New Street, Basingstoke.

Natural Science Society Museum, 39 Christchurch Road, Bournemouth.

Rothesay Museum, Bournemouth. (Collection of rarer modern coins retrieved from general circulation.)

Red House Museum, Quay Road, Christchurch.

Tudor House Museum, St. Michael's Square, Southampton. (Roman.)

City Museum, Winchester. (Roman; Winchester Mint.)

Herefordshire

Hereford Museum, Broad Street. (Roman, including the Llangarron Hoard; English.)

Hertfordshire

Village Museum, Ashwell, Baldock.

Hitchin Museum, Paynes Park, Hitchin.

Letchworth Museum and Art Gallery, Broadway, Letchworth.

Verulanium Museum, St. Michaels, St. Albans.

Kent

Borough Museum, Central Park, Dartford.

Borough Museum, Walnut Tree Road, Erith.

Folkestone Museum and Art Gallery, Grace Hill, Folkestone.
Maidstone Museum and Art Gallery, St. Faith Street, Maidstone.
(Roman, Saxon and Norman.)
Public Museum and Library, The Drive, Sevenoaks.
Municipal Museum, Mount Pleasant, Tunbridge Wells.

Lancashire

Public Library, Ramsden Square, Barrow-in-Furness.
Blackburn Public Library, Museum and Art Gallery, Library
Street, Blackburn.
Museum and Art Gallery, Civic Centre, Bolton 3.
Central Library and Museum, Oriel Road, Bootle.
Bury Museum, Manchester Road, Bury.
Lancaster Museum, Old Town Hall, Market Square, Lancaster.
Pennington Hall Museum and Art Gallery, Leigh.
Manchester Museum, University of Manchester.
Municipal Art Gallery and Museum, Union Street, Oldham.
Corporation Museum, Esplanade, Rochdale.
Public Museum, Central Library, St. Helens.
Public Library and Museum, Salford.
Atkinson Art Gallery, Lord Street, Southport.
Botanic Gardens Museum, Churchtown, Southport.

Leicestershire

City Museum and Art Gallery, New Walk, Leicester.
Loughborough Museum, Granby Street, Loughborough.
Archaeological and Historical Society, County Library, The
Square, Market Harborough.

Lincolnshire

Public Library, Grantham.
Doughty Museum, Town Hall Square, Grimsby.
City and County Museum, Broadgate, Lincoln. (Roman and
Saxon.)

London

Borough Museum, 232 Plumstead High Street, Plumstead, S.E.18.

British Museum, Department of Coins and Medals. (National Collection.)

Church Farm House Museum, Church End, N.W.4.

The Cuming Museum, Walworth Road, S.E.17.

The Horniman Museum, Forest Hill, S.E.23.

Islington Central Library, 68 Holloway Road, N.7.

Mocatta Museum, University College, Gower Street, W.C.1.

The Museum, Gunnersbury Park, W.3.

Southgate Museum, Broomfield Park, Palmers Green, N.13.

Middlesex

Public Library, Boston Manor Road, Brentford.

Hayes and Harlington Museum, County Library, Golden Crescent, Hayes.

County Library, High Street, Uxbridge.

Norfolk

Yarmouth Museum, 4 South Quay, Great Yarmouth.

Northumberland

Art Gallery and Museum, Marygate, Berwick-upon-Tweed.

Corstopitum Roman Museum, Corbridge.

Chesters Museum, Housesteads, Hexham.

Society of Antiquaries of Newcastle, Black Gate Museum, Newcastle upon Tyne.

Nottinghamshire

Mansfield Museum and Art Gallery, Leeming Street, Mansfield.

Municipal Museum, Appleton Gate, Newark-on-Trent. (Siege Pieces.)

City Museum and Art Gallery, Nottingham. (Roman.)

Worksop Public Library and Museum, Worksop.

Oxfordshire

Heberden Coin Room, Ashmolean Museum.

Shropshire

Trust Museum. (Roman; Shrewsbury Mint.)
Shrewsbury Museum. (Roman; Shrewsbury Mint.)

Somerset

Roman Baths Museum, Bath.
Victoria Art Gallery, Bath.
Kingswood School, Bath.
Admiral Blake Museum, Blake Street, Bridgwater.
Glastonbury Lake Village Museum, Glastonbury.
County Museum, Taunton Castle, Taunton. (Roman.)
Wells Museum, Cathedral Green, Wells.
Wyndham Museum, Yeovil.

Staffordshire

Stoke-on-Trent Museum and Art Gallery, Hanley. (Tutbury
    hoard; Lightwood Roman hoard.)
Public Library, Art Gallery and Museum, Bird Street, Lichfield.
Stafford Museum, The Green, Stafford.
Castle Museum, Holloway, Tamworth. (Tamworth Mint.)
Central Library and Art Gallery, Lichfield Street, Walsall.

Suffolk

Moyses Hall Museum, Bury St. Edmunds.
Ancient House Museum, White Hart Street, Ipswich.

Surrey

Godalming Museum, Charterhouse, Godalming.
Kingston-upon-Thames Museum, Fairfield Road, Kingston.

Sussex

Bognor Regis Museum Collection, c/o Clerk of the Council,
    Town Hall, Bognor Regis.

Hastings Museum, Hastings. (Anglo-Saxon and Norman pennies of Sussex Mints.)

Museum of Art, New Church Road, Hove.

Bodiam Castle, Bodiam, Robertsbridge.

Rye Museum, Watchbell House, Rye.

Warwickshire

Birmingham Museum.

Nuneaton Museum and Art Gallery, Riversley Park, Nuneaton.

Borough Library and Museum, Rugby.

Wiltshire

Avebury Museum, Avebury, Near Marlborough.

The Old Weigh House, Cricklade.

Devizes Museum, Long Street, Devizes. (Roman.)

Salisbury and South Wilts Museum, Ann Street, Salisbury.

Worcestershire

Dudley Museum, St. James' Road, Dudley.

Kidderminster Museum, Market Street, Kidderminster.

Public Library, Graham Road, Malvern.

Yorkshire

Bagshaw Museum and Art Gallery, Wilton Park, Batley.

Public Library, Art Gallery and Museum, Champney Road, Beverley.

Bolling Hall Museum, Bradford 4.

Cartwright Memorial Hall Museum, Bradford 9.

Bayle Museum, Bridlington.

Public Library and Art Gallery, Halifax Road, Brighouse.

Castleford Museum, Castleford.

Dewsbury Museum, Crownest Park, Dewsbury.

Doncaster Museum and Art Gallery, Doncaster.

Bankfield Museum, Halifax.

Royal Pump Room Museum, Crescent Road, Harrogate.

Tolson Memorial Museum, Ravensknowle Park, Huddersfield.

The Manor House Museum, Ilkley.
City Museum, Leeds. (Roman; Saxon; Norman; York Mint.)
Cliffe Castle Art Gallery and Museum, Keighley.
Municipal Museums, 23 High Street, Kingston-upon-Hull.
Municipal Museum, Clifton Park, Rotherham.
Sheffield Museum, Weston Park, Sheffield 10.
Craven Museum, Skipton.
City Museum, Wood Street, Wakefield.
Whitby Museum, Pannett Park, Whitby.
Ampleforth College Museum, Ampleforth College, York.
Castle Museum, York.
The Yorkshire Museum, York.

Isle of Wight

Museum of Isle of Wight Geology, Sandown.

IRELAND

Trinity College, Dublin.

SCOTLAND

National Museum of Antiquities, Edinburgh.
Royal Scottish Museum, Edinburgh.

WALES

National Library of Wales, Aberystwyth.
National Museum of Wales, Cardiff.

INDEX

Index

Index